The Numbered Motion Offense

by Mel Hankinson

© Copyright 1993
by Championship Books & Video Productions

All rights reserved.
No part of this book may be reproduced in any form or by any
means without permission in writing from the publisher.

ISBN 1-56404-05206

Printed in the United States of America

Championship Books & Video Productions
P.O. Box 1166 - ISU Station
Ames, Iowa 50010

About the Author

Mel Hankinson has been coaching basketball on the college level for more than 20 years. He began at Slippery Rock University, became the first assistant at the University of Iowa and presently serves as the athletic director and head basketball coach at The Master's College. He has coached more than 15 championship teams, with one advancing to the College Division "Final Four." In addition, he has been named "Coach of the Year" on seven different occasions. Mr. Hankinson has spoken at hundreds of clinics, banquets, and commencements, both nationally and internationally. These include engagements at the 1990 "Final Four Coaches Clinic" in Denver, the "Sport Psychology Institute" in Chicago, the "Super Cup" in Dortmund, Germany, the "Mediterranean Games" in Athens, Greece, and the "International Basketball Academy" in Pula, Yugoslavia.

More importantly, Mel Hankinson is one of the leading basketball writers and producers of teaching videos in the nation. Presently, over 2,500 colleges and universities are using his texts or videos in their classrooms with their teams (see Appendix A for a list of Mel Hankinson's books and tapes). His new works include: *Bench Coaching - Defensive Strategy*, *Developing Championship Thinking*, and *The Millwright Poet*.

J.C. Cherry
Editor - In - Chief

Table of Contents

Preface		vii
Forward		ix
Introduction		xi
Chapter 1	What is the Numbered Motion Offense?	1
Chapter 2	The Nature of the Numbered Motion Offense	5
Chapter 3	The Purpose of the Numbered Motion Offense	10
Chapter 4	The Function of the Numbered Motion Offense	14
Chapter 5	Teaching the Numbered Motion Offense	35
Chapter 6	The Fastbreak and the Numbered Motion Offense	56
Chapter 7	Attacking Zone Defenses with the Numbered Motion Offense	63
Chapter 8	To the Bewildered and Beguiled Critic of the Numbered Motion Offense	72
Chapter 9	Signaling the Numbered Motion Offense	78
Chapter 10	Making Basketball Fun with the Numbered Motion Offense	82
	Index	88

Preface

The *Numbered Motion Offense* is not written for the novice coach. A prerequisite for reading the text would be to have a thorough understanding of the motion offense. Mel Hankinson, Athletic Director and Basketball Coach of the Master's College has written an excellent book, *Progressions for Teaching Basketball*, on the basics of the motion game. The reader is encouraged to have a thorough understanding of the basic concepts of the motion game before venturing into the numbered motion.

J.C. Cherry
Editor's Note

Forward

In the early 1970's, Dean Smith, the head basketball coach at the University of North Carolina, was credited with popularizing the "motion offense." Coaches have used a wide variety of adaptations to the motion's concept, which include set plays leading into the motions flow and delay breaks with automatic entries which include designed special offensive role opportunities that follow with motion action. Some have confined the responsibilities of designated pickers, rebounders, shooters and non-shooters while broadening the creativity of each coach's imagination as he attempted to control the uncertainty of the motion action. Today, coaches continue searching for ways to give the motion consistency and predictability within its flow.

The blessing of the uncertainty of players' movement within the motion has also been its curse. Coaches like the freedom to have players read and counter pressure defenses, but cringe when their players make poor offensive choices that have in many instances cost them the game.

The *Numbered Motion Offense* combines the basic two man game action in a controlled motion that enhances the predictability of motion function for a high percentage shot during the pressure phase of the offense. As a pragmatic coach and not a prophet, the author sees the vast majority of successful teams using the numbered motion as their basic offense within the next few years. "If you don't use it, you'll be beaten by it!"[1]

---

[1] Del Harris, the former coach of the Milwaukee Bucks, has written an excellent booklet entitled, *Bucks Motion Numbers Game*. The author would highly recommend anyone interested in pursuing motion concepts to contact Del regarding his innovative book. This text was a springboard from Del's idea and several other colleagues (Dean Smith, Bob Knight, Dale Clayton, Al LeFlorce, Phil Worrell, and Marty Street).

x

Introduction

The most often asked question since the advent of the motion offense is: "How may I control specific action within the midst of the offense?" The *Numbered Motion Offense* clearly offers the coach that control.

Critics will be quick to complain that the offense is too complicated. However, the author has observed this system of play used effectively by junior high teams as well as teams in the National Basketball Association. Conversely, instead of complicating the game, it simplifies the offense by providing the coach with effective communicative verbal "cues" for enhancing and evaluating the fundamental skill performance of his team.

The *Numbered Motion Offense* is innovative and builds on one's present offensive system of play. Furthermore, its versatility permits the coach to not only play with the traditional personnel line-up of two guards, two forwards, and a center, but the numbers permit combinations which range from five guards to five centers!

It's exciting to be on the "cutting edge" of an innovative offense that will improve your offensive coaching techniques, maximize your players' fundamental skill level, and raise the offensive efficiency of your team!

Chapter 1

What is the Numbered Motion Offense?

Chapter #1
What is the Numbered Motion Offense?

"Necessity" has often been the "mother of invention," and some cures have been less desirable than the illness. Such has been the nature of the motion offenses since their inception in the early 1970's. The motion was introduced primarily to neutralize pressure defensive tactics which were destroying set plays and shuffle offensive systems popular in that period. In the motion, offensive players were taught how to read various defined schemes and counteract correspondingly. The motion offense often cured many defensive problems, however its side-effects brought on new illnesses. Although defensive pressure lessened, coaches lost much of the control over shot selection, players staying within their offensive roles, critical end-game action, plus "congestion" around the basket, which gave the motion a new name - "the 15 foot jump shot offense."

For the past ten years, coaches have sought various methods for gaining control of the offense, yet maintaining the motion's flow. This has been done unsatisfactorily by using "delay fast break options", "set plays", "crutch - end of the game plays", designated pickers and/or shooters, and "combination motion, flex or fixed play sets" which return the offense to basic motion action should any or all of these combinations fail. The question of how to maintain control amid the flow of the offense has been answered by the *Numbered Motion Offense*.

Numbers are given to every offensive action that takes place in the game of basketball. Progressively this begins with all cutting movements (straight cuts, V cuts, etc.), adds critical fundamental skills necessary (individual offensive moves, picking, passing, dribbling, shooting, rebounding, etc.), then incorporates these fundamental skills with one-on-one isolations, two man games between guards, forwards and the center. Combinations depend on the coach's personnel and game situations. The team may use numbers which combine guard-guard, guard-center, etc., to meet a particular game need; three man games make the offensive even more complex to defend by adding any number of guard, forward, center combinations. Ninety percent of the numbered motion offense involves 2 and/or 3 man games with the 4th and 5th man playing supportive roles. However, if the coach has a small team, he may use a 4 or 5 man motion offensive set; therefore, initially all of the fundamental skills critical for the efficient functioning of the numbered motion offense are identified.

Second, the numbered motion offense is integrated with a fastbreak system. It doesn't matter what kind of system a coach's team employs: sideline, numbered, or a quick combination release, a slow down, or a standard break; the numbered motion offense is easily incorporated in all fastbreak systems of play.

Third, the numbered motion offense may be used after a dead ball, made basket or broken fastbreak. It is also of particular value in quick 2-on-2, 3-on-3, or 4-on-4 transition situations which gives organized attack "cues" to the offense as they take advantage of the extra floor space available by the retreating defense.

Fourth, a coach and his team may use the numbers in the mid-motion to free a player who is "hot," take advantage of a player who is in foul trouble or is in a mismatch situation due to speed or size.

Fifth, strategically, once the players understand the numbers, they (or the coach) may create various entries or crutch plays in the midst of the offensive flow. This forces the defense to adjust to a myriad of offensive alignments which include front picks, vertical and horizontal picks, down picks (all picks may be single, double, even triple walled, or staggered), floor spread, single, double, triple stacks, etc.; these are all available by using the numbered motion offense.

Sixth, one of the greatest advantages of the numbered motion offense is to be able to repeatedly attack the defense at its most vulnerable point. Conversely, if the offense has an over-riding strength gained by a particular phase of the number series, then that aspect may continually be used to exploit the defense.

Seventh, by using the numbered motion offense, the coach increases his chances of winning the tightly contested "end games" (the last five minutes of the contest). When a number or numbers are called, unlike in the basic motion game, the coach and players know what should happen in the entry, mid, and final phase of the offense. If there is a breakdown in any phase, the offense continues with specific counters designed for the high percentage score. Each player's role, shot choices, and rebound responsibilities have been identified and practiced so there is a high level of confidence among the coaches and team during critical "end game" situations.

Finally, because the numbered offense has a great deal of structure within its freedom of movement, the offense may be quickly evaluated as to why its "parts" or "whole" succeeded or failed.

To recap, the numbered motion offense differs from the basic motion in that it provides greater development of fundamental skills by sharpening communication between student and teacher; second, it enhances the fastbreak game by permitting a more fluid transition from the delay break into the numbered motion offense; third, much of basketball is played in transitional phases, thus permitting offensive players specific options when they find themselves 2-on-2, 3-on-3, 4-on-4, etc.; fourth, players who are "hot" are more likely to receive the ball because the entire team is looking to get the "scorer" open by setting single, double, or even triple picks; at the same time, their scoring opportunity is increased because within the numbered system they are looking for the "high percentage" shot; fifth, the defense must adjust to a wider variety of offensive attack alignments; sixth, the offense may use its specific strength while attacking a particular weakness in the defense; seventh, because of the ability of the coaches and players to control what is happening on the court, the "end game" has a greater opportunity to succeed because of planning rather than "chance;" finally, the coach and the team can objectively evaluate the offense's efficiency more expediently.

Chapter 2

Nature of the Numbered Motion Offense

Chapter 2
Nature of the Numbered Motion Offense

One of the greatest errors any opponent can make in battle is to think that they have a "secret weapon" that is capable of winning the day without tireless effort placed on peaking one's skills for the event. "Work is the price for freedom." American Stealth bombers delivered their payloads with pinpoint accuracy during the Gulf War because they had spent thousands of hours "paying the price" of perfecting their rocket deliveries. The numbered motion offense may hit the enemy with the surprise of a Stealth Bomber, but after initial impact, its continued success will be dependent on the execution of the offensive fundamental basics of the game.

The "constants" which need to be considered when building toward the numbered motion game are:

1. Does everyone have an opportunity to score?

2. Are your best offensive players getting the ball so they can score?

3. Do all players know their offensive strengths and limitations?

4. Are players getting the ball **where** they can score?

5. How can we hide weaknesses and emphasize strengths of our various players?

6. Is the offense **terminal** or can we maintain a **continuity** of movement once the defense has shut down our initial set?

7. Are our strong rebounders in a position from the offense to get the second shot?

8. Who is responsible for being back on defense?

9. Can we get into our offense from our fast break?

10. Does the offensive set help recognize the kind of defense that we are facing?

11. Does our offense work against a man-to-man and/or a zone?

12. Does our offense work against a combination man-to-man zone?

13. Does our offense include most or all of the possible methods of scoring?

14. Does our offense have flexible alternatives should a defensive team be causing us problems?

15. Are all players **without** the ball moving with purpose?

16. Does our offense compliment our defense?

17. Is the offense designed for our team or my ego?

18. Do I know the fundamentals that need to be developed for the offense to be effective?

19. Are we teaching patterns or the development of fundamental skills?

20. Is the offense simply a popular product of the times or is it based on sound basketball principles?

In the next teaching progression, restate reasons to your team why your present motion offense has been an effective offensive weapon. (The author encourages the reader to contact Dean Smith, at the University of North Carolina, or Bob Knight, at Indiana University, on the various aspects of the motion offense.)

1. There is no pattern employed (the defense cannot pressure specific areas).

2. The offense is not terminal; therefore, you do not have to reset after the defense stops the action.

3. All five players are continually moving.

4. It can be used by any tempo you choose to play.

5. The sets can be modified to suit your personnel.

6. The offense can be used against zones or man-to-man defenses.

7. It's difficult to scout because of its variety of patterns.

Continue with the offensive progression in teaching by insisting that your team understands the concept of the motion rather than specific rules:

1. Generally do not pick on the ball (unless it is a forward-guard or center-guard pick).

2. Pick away from the ball when possible.

3. Maintain 15 to 18 spacing on the perimeter.

4. Fill the high post if it is vacant.

5. Never make two consecutive cuts in the same direction.

6. Never go behind the man to receive the return pass.

7. Always occupy the defensive man.

8. Use of the dribble:
    A. To improve passing angles
    B. To take the ball to the basket
    C. To move the ball against full court pressure

9. Post play (low post rules):
    A. Back pick for a perimeter man when ball is reversed
    B. Pick for the high post man on ball reversal
    C. Pick across the man in the low post
    D. Use a screen by a high post player

E. Roll on a feed from the high post

   F. When the high post is open, fill it

   G. Be an efficient passer - inside, weakside, guard-forward post reaction

10. Post play (high post rules):

   A. Always be on the ball side

   B. Screen down for low posts

   C. Post pick for the perimeter player

11. If you have nowhere to go, replace yourself.

12. Many coaches do not set up, but go directly into the motion game off their last pass on the fastbreak.

There are unlimited possibilities concerning various plays available to a team using a motion offense. However, as the author indicated in the introduction, this text assumes that the reader has an understanding of the "basics" of the motion offense.

The nature of the numbered motion offense is to take the basic motion offensive constants and add a separate numbering system to these concepts for communication and control.

Chapter 3

Purpose of the Numbered Motion Offense

Chapter 3
Purpose of the Numbered Motion Offense

In Chapters 1 and 2, the author described the similarities between the basic motion game and the numbered motion offense. However, now we must recognize the subtle, yet significant differences between their functions. Be reminded that the primary purpose of the numbered system is to bring the flow under the control of both player and coach. The numbered motion offense is distinct from the basic motion offense:

1. Foremost, the numbers enhance communication between the coach and players regarding the specific action that must take place on the court. Execution of team and individual movement is demanded by the numbered called. Rather than a coach yelling, "Move, move, move!" and players crying, "Where, where, where?" or "Why, why, why?", the coach or players offer a fundamental skills number for function. This gives everyone purpose and direction eliminating the mentality of the courier who "saddled his horse and road off in all directions." The numbered motion offense directs specific movement on command amid the motion. If there is a lack of motion, or error of execution, this is quickly recognized by both player and coach.

2. Next, it dictates who will be passing, picking, and shooting the ball in relationship to time and score.

3. Philosophically, it encourages team play. Because of the teaching of verbals, players will have more of an opportunity to understand why they are moving where they are moving for individual and/or team purposes.

The economist, Dr. Douglas McGregor often compares the two patterns of thinking of the authoritarian (Theory X) and the authoritative (Theory Y) method. Theory X proponents expound the belief that man is basically lazy and that he needs to be coerced, threatened, and manipulated to produce to his maximum level. Theory Y's position states that if man is given direction such that he can understand how to achieve specific goals that he will attain great levels of success. Dr. McGregor obviously concludes that the Theory Y workers achieve much higher levels of function because they understand the purpose of their mission and are intrinsically motivated to achieve identified targets.

Such is true with the numbered motion offense. It helps eliminate the oblique periods during the mid motion action when coach and player become apprehensive spectators anxiously hoping that something good will happen. Conversely, compare the exactness of execution when a number is called:

A. The offensive player will tend to work harder to get open because:
   (1) he knows that the entire team is trying to get him the ball.
   (2) he knows that if his teammates miss him on the first series of options they will continue to try to free him.
   (3) he knows, most importantly, that he doesn't have to shoot the ball the first time he receives it. Once his designated number is called, he's "it" for this series. Therefore, if he doesn't like the offensive opportunities when he receives the ball, he knows that in a short time his teammates will create another shot for him as soon as he gives up the ball. Obviously, this type of play encourages every player to give himself up to another member of the team. This mentally aids the star performer from "forcing" shots, and frustrates the defensive "ace" who is trying to stop your numbered scorer. Also, once a player's number is called the man guarding the called number is "it." If the defensive team doesn't switch, the single defender will be in for a very "bruising" evening.

B. It is the optimum time to teach him how to apply the fundamental skills that he has been developing at the "parts" breakdown station and use them in a "whole" game situation. Few times will you see an individual exercise greater concentration, execute more efficiently, or give maximum effort than when "his" number is called.

4. A higher level of confidence may be built when using the numbered motion offense in team and individual play:

   A. Purpose of role is more clearly identified for individuals and team members.

   B. Purpose for exploiting any defensive counters has been practiced and is anticipated.

   C. Purpose for being patient is built into the offense regarding passing, dribbling, rebounding, and shooting in relationship to time and score.

D. Purpose has been articulated for the exactness of team and individual function in a "tight" game. Therefore, the level of performance execution has been raised.

Finally, Proverbs 29:18 teaches us "where there is no vision the people perish." Continued studies have revealed that those individuals and corporations who know "where" they are going, "why" they are going there, and "how" to get to their destination usually arrive. This gives a more defined purpose to their aims and goals. Similarly, the numbered motion offense refines the basic motion set by giving its "parts" greater definition as to how they fit into the "whole." As has been described, articulation of function enhances performance by giving it definitive purpose.

Chapter 4

Function of the Numbered Motion Offense

Chapter #4
Function of the Numbered Motion Offense

In this section, the basic numbers used in the numbered motion offense will be identified, their function described, how numbers may be combined in a systematic order articulated, and various time and score situations for game application presented.

Del Harris, in his *Milwaukee Bucks Offensive System* booklet, began building his offensive series with the number 6. Numbers 1 through 5 were saved for special "crutch" plays to be used with personnel strengths or for timely baskets in critical situations. Therefore, our series begins with the number 6 and is built on Del's basic system 6 through 18.

Specific identification of the numbers and their function are as follows:

"6"   Screening up or down; 6 up is a backpick and 6 down is a frontpick.

"7"   Pick and roll action.

"70" Pick and roll play where the big man handles the ball and passes it to the small man. The main actions are "Big on Little" or "Little on Big."

"8"   Backdoors, early release on a pick/roll, (7 or 70) plus 6's or 12's. Secondly, "8" may be called for a backdoor open cut series if the defensive pressure is fully extended. "8" also creates many give and go situations because of an extended defense.

"9"   Stack action involving 2, 3, or 4 offensive players. Stack action may include curls, "pop in," "pop out," pick the picker, etc.

"10" Curls - On any elbow, or at a middle or low post downpick, the offensive team may use the curl option. The man who sets the downpick will pop back as the low man curls. Use the principle "little" picking for "big" or "big" picking for "little" in this game action.

"11" One-on-one isolation action.

"12" Horizontal or diagonal post picking (this may be from the low, mid, high, or short corner positions). Primary movement is to have the ballside player pick to the weakside of the court for the opposite man. "12R" reverses this picking order by having the weakside man pick the ballside post at any time.

"13" Any lob pass action.

"14" Snapback action. The ballhandler on top draws the defense with him and then snaps the ball back to the opposite wing for a shot or post feed.

"15" Drive, draw, and kick.

"16" Perimeter weakside or strongside blind pick action.

"17" Any combination of 7, 70, and 6 action where 7 or 70 is followed by a 6. Pick the picker option.

"18" Any combination of 12 and 6 action where a 12 is followed by a 6. Another "pick the picker" move.

In addition to these numbers, players are numbered by their positions:
- "1" point guard
- "2" second guard
- "3" big guard or small forward
- "4" power forward
- "5" center

One should not become overly concerned with the position structure. For instance, with numbered motion, a coach may use four point guards or four forwards; the numbers are simply to describe the movement of five players on the court. (Historically, teams have identified their squads in this fashion.)

These numbers serve as the foundation for the numbered motion offense. We now move to the most exciting phase of the offense - combining these primary numbers in systematic order based on the strengths of the team's personnel. A coach is limited only by his creativity and talent, and by the level of understanding of the players![1]

The author suggests the following "conceptual" numbers rather than listing a myriad of optional numbers so that the offense may be more clearly understood.

"6" Defined as a screen up or a screen down. Let's look at some fun we may have taking the number 6 and combining it with some other numbers.

1. "6" - Screening up or down is an offense in itself. Be reminded of the many fundamental options that may take place in these two man games: front and back screens, fake back screens, "bumps," pick then reverse to and from the basket, pick and "slip cut" to the basket, plus backdoor quick cuts are all basic options to be taught from the number 6.

2. Now let's combine the number "6" screening concept with the number "2" player position which was described earlier in the chapter. If "62" is called, all players know they will be setting down and up screens for the 2 man. The first number 6 alerts the players as to the offensive number concept to be used; the second number, in this case 2, communicates that 2 is the primary player that all team members are trying to free for a high or good percentage shot.[2] (High and good percentage shots are designated by a player's skill level and the time and score left on the game.) Secondary players are identified as players 1, 3, 4, 5 if the number "62" is called. Obviously, if the number "63" is called, then players 1, 2, 4, 5 become secondary players. It is important to note that generally secondary players are only permitted to take high percentage shots if their number is not called. This is a critical aspect of the offense in order to maintain a rhythmic flow, and to permit all team members to be continually involved with the offense as threats to score. Now, when a player's number is called (for an example, 62):

---

[1] "We tend to over-coach and under-teach." Caution should be given in this phase of the offense. If the coach becomes enamored by the limitless options the offense offers or players become absorbed by memorizing motion numbers, the result will be disastrous: inefficient movement with dysfunctional execution.

[2] A high percentage shot is one taken in a specific area by a player that can make that shot at least 80% of the time. A good percentage shot is defined as a shot that is taken by the player from a specific area can be made 50% of the time.

A. He tends to execute the fundamentals of getting open more efficiently in order to receive the ball.

B. His teammates seem to execute their fundamentals of picking, pivoting, cutting, dribbling, etc. more effectively in order to increase 2's opportunity to receive the ball.[3]

C. If 2 doesn't receive the ball such that he has a high or good percentage shot (depending on time, score, tempo, flow, etc.), then the "6" motion of down and back screens continues with the principles of the offense continuing as previously discussed. It should be noted that 2 will be receiving single, double, triple post screens, staggered screens and "walled" screens. He may go over the top or bottom, curl, etc.; cut from the "inside-out" toward the sideline, or break from the "outside-in" toward the basket to receive the ball. All four of 2's teammates are "ganging-up" on the man defending him. One player remarked that, "We are going to make 2's defender pay for guarding him so closely."

D. Communication enhances function. When "62" is called, everyone knows their role and exactly what they should do because of the exactness of the verbal command and the demand for specific function.

E. The called number gives the coach greater control of players' functions within the motion. If "62" is called our primary function is to get 2 open for a good or high percentage shot. This structure is obviously more effective than saying, "Get Bob open anyway you can, and none of you others guys shoot the ball unless you have a lay-up." As one can see, the coach may design as much control as he chooses within the numbered system. In some instances, with regard to time, score, and personnel, the coach may insist on designated shooter(s), picker(s), passer(s), etc. Usually, the more limited the talent level, the more structure that needs to be added to increase the team's opportunity for success.

---

[3]The team must be taught to keep the flow of the offense going once a player's number is called. If this is not taught, a "forced" offense will result in foolish turnovers.

"7"   Pick and roll action gives the defense another set of spacing, mismatches, picks, and backdoor offensive angles the offense can try to counter. Players are instructed to use the "Big on Little" or "Little on Big" principle when picking and rolling in their five man game. The picker may "reverse" pivot, or snap his head and "quick cut" to the basket before or after setting the pick on the defensive man. Let's look at some basic options we may use with 7:

1. First, we may spread the floor and run a five man motion offense of "nothing but 7's." Players on and off the ball are running pick and rolls, staying aware of spacing, ball location, moving with purpose, and their function while eliminating congestion. ("70," which is passing from guard to post man, is an integral part of this two man "Big-Little" and "Little-Big" maneuver. 70 is particularly valuable in the delay fast break phase of a team's offense, or in a 3 on 3, 4 on 4 quick transition game.

2. If we want to add down screens and back picks (6) to our pick and roll (7) offensive series, we simply call "67." Players on and off the ball are opening the floor, reading the defense, and using the previous principles discussed in 6's and 7's to secure a high or good percentage shot in relationship to time and score.

3. Now, should we have a 4 man who is great at running a pick and roll, and a 5 man who we want to hide, then we take more control of the offense and call "74" ("7" for the pick and roll, and "4" to designate the picker). If we want 4 to pick for everyone, we call "740." In this case, "0" stands for "all." If we want 4 to pick and roll continuously with 2, then we would call "742". All players would be picking and rolling looking for the high percentage shot. However, our primary action is the pick and roll (7) between 4 and 2.

   If you really want to see your opponents scratch their heads, call "6742." "6" tells us that we are going to be down and back screening. If we are not down screening, then we are running pick and rolls (7). But our highest priority structured play is the pick and roll (7) between our 4 and 2 man. Thus, "6742."

4. If we want to hide 5 in mid game, and run a series of pick and roll options with 4, 1, 2, and 3, then our verbal cue is "744." (First, the 5 man has been given whatever rebounding, picking, etc. responsibilities that the coach has chosen.) 7 denotes pick

and roll action. A <u>double</u> 4 indicates that 4 is the "main man" and will be picking on and off the ball for 1, 2, and 3, and be rolling hard to the basket. We are looking for all the post up, drive spreads, inside passing, and short jump shots which will occur with this action. These same principles apply if we have an outstanding 5 player. In this case, the verbal call would be "755." In rare instances, the coach may have two great 4 and 5 men where a "745" may be used effectively.

"8" Backdoors, early release on a pick/roll, (7 or 70) plus 6's or 12's. 8 continues to enhance offensive communication while giving the coach more control over the motion game:

1. A straight call "8" has players: spreading the floor (which automatically lessens basket congestion), down and up picking with 6's, pick and rolling with 7's and horizontally picking with 12's. They primarily will be looking for backdoor baskets from these various offensive movements. "8" is great at: protecting a lead, controlling tempo, running the clock down to set up a special shot, or countering an extended pressure defense.

2. "85" or "84" means that we are looking for the backdoor cut from 5 or 4 from their operative areas in the high post or from the short 15 foot shooting spots in the corners. If a 5 or 4 misses the lob or pass on the straight cut, they may position themselves securely in the low post position, sprint to the "short corner," set in "pinch post" position, or look to run a "give-and-go" with the 1, 2, or 3.

3. "812" has the 4 or 5 operating in the mid post to the "short corner," appearing to set horizontal or diagonal picks for one another. However, both are moving quickly, creating space for one another and looking for the backdoor cut and/or "give-and-go" with the guard.

4. "845" brings 4 and 5 to the high post, spreading guards 1, 2, and 3 wide on the court. A guard sets up the series by passing to 4 or 5. While the ball is in the air to one of the big men, the other big man cuts backdoor sharply to the basket. This will often result in a post to post touch pass for an easy lay-up. If the ball is entered on the wing, the strongside post drops to the mid post and the weakside post stays high, looking for the backdoor cut from the guard or the low post. The weakside post

looks for the backdoor option if the ball is passed into the low post. Conversely, the low post looks for the same "touch pass options" if the ball is passed to the weakside high post teammate.

5. "862" would mean that we are going to run a backdoor (8) after we have cleared one half the court, with a down screen or back pick for 2. This, of course, could be used with any other player on the court ("861, 863, 864, 865" - the same principles apply).

6. "872" would mean that we are going to run a backdoor (8) after clearing one side of the floor with a pick and roll for 2. (Once again this may be done with any combination of players - "871, 873, 874, 875.") If 4's or 5's number is called, they become the backdoor cutter rather than 1, 2, or 3. (There will be many instances where the coach will want to exploit a "slow" 4 or 5 defensive player. This series will permit that to happen.)

7. "841" means that we are going to run a backdoor "give-and-go" (8) with a power forward (4) and the point guard (1). This is excellent action against defensive pressure and will result in straight cut "give-and-go" baskets and/or "blind pigs" from the weakside of the floor. If the coach wants to give more freedom to the motion and add a 5 man, then he may share with the players that "8" means we are looking for the backdoor for the "give-and-go" off 5 or 4. (5 and 4's primary operative positions are in the "pinch post." Once again, this permits the wing guards room for "blind pig" cuts from the weakside of the court.)

"9"   Refers to stack action involving 2, 3, or 4 offensive players who stack then curl, using pop "in" and "outs," shuffle cuts, etc. to get open. Stacks are one of the least talked about, but most used weapons by coaches who like the tempo of a slow controlled game. In the numbered motion offensive system of play, the stack may be used after a made basket, a dead ball, in a "crutch" play situation, or to create another look for the defense. The multiplicity of counters which must be adjusted to by the defense is a textbook in itself. However, in this section, rather than go into an in-depth study of the stack offensive options, the author will show how stacks are used to compliment the numbered motion game. We will identify and give the number function for the single, double, triple, and quadruple regular stacks. Then we will see that by simply inverting the stacks, the defense must adjust to a radically different kind of offensive movement.

Here are a couple of key teaching points about gaining the most effective use of the stack. In the regular stack (double, triple, or quadruple), teach the biggest player to line up on the top of the stack. Secondly, have the player buried "deepest" in the stack move first. Thirdly, all other players move in relationship to their offensive teammate and how the defensive team reacts to the offensive movements. As a teaching tool, tape various stack alignment positions on the court. (This will vary from high, low, mid, and corner positions.) By changing the offensive team's alignment position, one changes the defensive team's angles for defending the stack options. The effect is like adding several offensive plays. The coach is encouraged to be creative with vertical, horizontal, and even diagonal stacks without compromising fundamental skill movements. Always remind the players that there are no short cuts to developing an efficient offense. Teamwork, fundamental execution, timing, and striving for perfection in the exactness of intensive movement are the keys to making an effective stack offense work successfully.

1. When "9" is called, the players are in a single stack offense. In most instances, 5 or 4 is at the top position on the stack (they are also responsible for its location on the court). The coach has shown the post man the three most advantageous location angles on the court and should expect them to line up on those corresponding angles. If the post is lining up incorrectly, or if the coach would like to have the big men in a particular area because of time or score, then the coach may shout: "high, middle or pinch post left or right," ensuring their proper alignment. Then, 2 or 3 guard stacks behind the 5 or 4 man. If 2 moves into the stack with 5, 3 sets wide on either wing, and 4 moves to his power forward designated area. 4's primary areas depend on his skills. If he is a good perimeter shooter, then he should play more like a 3 guard rather than a power forward. However, if he is more of a center or power forward, then he should "mirror" 5's position and operate approximately 15 feet from the basket. In most instances when "9" is called, 1 is bringing the ball down the court, 5 and 2 are at mid post, 3 is on either wing and 4 is in the short corner away from 5 and 2.

   If 2 is the "designator," then everyone keys their movement after 2 moves. Once 2 begins his two man game with 5 and 3, then 4 responds accordingly with all of the two man games that everyone must teach their players in the motion offense. If 2 holds up a "fist" (or the coach signals to 2 with a "fist" sign), he then waits for 3 to come off the stack before making his move. "3" may make a shuffle, cut low or high, cut from the baseline and receive a wall screen then curl or V-cut back to the corner. He also has the option of returning to the weakside of the court and playing two man games with 4.

If 2 raises his hand instead of a fist, then he will be initiating the stack offense and is looking to play two man games with 5, then 3 or 4.

Once these initial movements are made in "9," then the players continue the number motion options that we described with numbers 6, 7, and 8.

2. If "59" is called by the 4 or 5 man, then 2 and/or 3 set on the high side with 4 or 5 setting low. This gives the defense another set of offensive movements to contend with. It should be noted that 2 and 3 still maintain the prerogative to hold up a fist, open hand, or no hand at all (if no hand is raised, then either 2 or 3 initiates the offense while the other players move from their reads). Please note that even though they are on the high side, they are still responsible for starting the two man game.

3. "29" indicates that we are going to initiate the numbered motion offense with a double stack.

   A. Alignment should be consistent with the order of the stack: 5 and 4 are high and 2 and 3 are low.

   B. Location on the floor will vary with each stack. "2" and 3 are "married" to 5 and 4, so they must line up wherever they take them. "5" and 4 are taught the low, mid, high post, or short corner primary operating areas. "2" and 3 may move to the top of the double stack by shouting to 5 and 4, "29R." They still follow the post man's area location and initiate the offense by moving first. Once again, this gives the defensive team another set of angle and player movements to defend.

   C. It is best to initiate the offense with a "designator." In most instances, 2 or 3 is the "designator" and he keys the offense with a raised fist, open hand, and/or first cut movement. The multiplicity of double stack designator options are an offense unto themselves. However, the coach must be cautioned of players or teams with a quick shot offensive temperament that does not permit the defense to guard the basket less than 10 seconds. In mid-game play, the offense needs to wear down the defense with patient execution.

D. Now the fun begins! Each coach examines his personnel and the numbers presented to build his own offense around the strengths and weaknesses of his players. There is no limit as to what the creative coach may design. Here is a sampling of how the numbered system fits together:

(1) "296" - a double stack (29) then continuous up and down screens (6).

(2) "297" - a double stack (29) then continuous pick and roll action (7).

(3) "298" - a double stack (29) then continuous back door action (8).

(4) "2962" - a double stack (29) with continuous up and down screens (6) for the 2 man (2).

(5) "2974" - a double stack (29) with continuous pick and roll screens (7) exclusively for the 4 man (4).

(6) "2985" - a double stack (29) with continuous back door action (8) for the 5 man (5).

[Note: To memorize the numbers without understanding the system will overwhelm the reader and the players. Therefore, as one learns how each number fits into the overall pattern, the "numbered motion" becomes a very simple set of concepts and the emphasis returns to fundamental execution of the identified systematic concept. Even movement such as "29872" ("29" - double stack, "8" - backdoor, "7" - pick and roll, "2" - designator) no longer paralyzes the mind, and gives the coach great control of the offensive movement.]

4. "39" indicates that we are going to initiate the offense with a triple stack:

A. Alignment will once again consist of the higher player number 5 setting high and the lowest number, in this case 2 or 3, setting low. The stack formation would be 5,4,3 or 5,4,2. (Because many coaches have great similarities between 5's and 4's skills, their position may be reversed, 4,5,3 or 4,5,2, without any bench call adjustment.)

B. Location of the triple stack (low, mid, high, or short corner) will be determined by the coaches, the player's call, the post man's positioning, or by a particular need in relation to time and score.

C. The "designator" who initiates the offense will be 2 or 3 to maintain consistency in the system's function. He will use a raised fist, open hand, and/or first cut movement to begin the offense.

D. Coaches should select combinations which best fit their personnel. If consistency within the system is to be maintained then:
   (1) "396" - a triple stack (39) then continuous up and down screens (6).
   (2) "397" - a triple stack (39) then continuous pick and roll action (7).
   (3) "398" - a triple stack (39) then continuous back door action (8).

If we continued building on the numbered system as we did on the double stack then:
   (4) "3962" - a triple stack (39) with continuous up and down screens (6) for the 2 man (2).
   (5) "3974" - a triple stack (39) with continuous pick and roll screens (7) exclusively for the 4 man (4).
   (6) "3985" - a triple stack (39) with continuous back door action (8) for the 5 man (5).

The author continues to reinforce in the mind of the reader that once the system is understood, the numbers may be easily applied.

5. "49" indicates that we are going to initiate the numbered motion offense with a quadruple stack.

   A. Alignment may be adjusted within the system to maximize function:
      (1) To be consistent with the higher to lower numbered alignment premise, our players would stack in a 5, 4, 3, 2 formation.
      (2) However, the coach has the prerogative within the system of having 2 and 3 mix within the stack behind 4 and 5. The stack may then read 5, 3, 4, 2 with 2 initiating the action.

(3) Since both 5's and 4's skills (along with 2 and 3) are often interchangeable, the coach may permit any combination of the players to reverse their positions. Therefore, it may read 4, 2, 5, 3 or 4, 3, 5, 2 with the lower numbered player initiating the movement.

B. Location of the stack (low, mid, high, or short corner) will be determined by: the coaches, the player's call, the post man's positioning or by a particular need in relation to time and score.

C. As in the triple stack, the designator will be 2 or 3, initiating movement with a raised fist, open hand, and/or first cut movement to begin the offense.

D. Combinations that may be used with the triple stack include the same initial options as the double and triple stacks: "496," "497," and "498." (See double stacks: "296," "297," "298," and the triple stacks "396," "397," "498" in the preceding paragraphs for their function.) Also the four digit numbers of the double and triple stacks apply to the quadruple stack. "4962," "4974," and 4985" are the same movements as the double and triple stacks once the entries have been indicated.

Hopefully, the author has been able to clearly articulate how the various stacks (9, 29, 39, and 49) easily fit with the 6, 7, and 8 actions of the numbered motion offensive system. Insist that the players not waste their energy memorizing numbers, but learn how these numbers function; this will increase their understanding of the game of basketball as well as enhance the efficiency of the offense.

"10" Curls - On any elbow, middle or low post downpick, the offensive team may use the curl option. The man who sets the downpick will pop back as the low man curls. We use the principle "little" picking for "big" or "big" picking for "little" in this game action:

1. Alignment will be adjusted to maximize the personnel and function:

    A. All stack action (9, 29, 39, and 49) are excellent entries into "10." Therefore, the coach may call:
    (1) "910" - single stack (9) into curl action (10).

- (2) "2910" - double stack (29) into curl action (10).
- (3) "3910" - triple stack (39) into curl action (10).
- (4) "4910" - quadruple stack (49) into curl action (10).

    B. The second most used number is 8 into 10 (810). "8" (back door series) extends any offensive player beyond the three point shooting line. This initial movement is particularly effective because 8 brings the defensive post man away from the basket, then the 10 movement takes him to the designated pick area. Most big men do not adjust well defensively to this expanded court coverage and therefore are easier to pick.

2. Location of the curl action pick must be identified as low, mid, or high. This will depend on strategy, time, and score.

3. Combinations. Since the primary purpose of 10 is to have the numbered motion continuously picking "little on big" and taking advantage of the mismatches inside and outside, the stack action (9's) and back door actions (8's) are clearly the best numbers to use in this series. However, pick and roll action (7's) after the guard and forward switch creates major adjustments for the defensive team. The author would encourage the reader to explore the wealth of possibilities available in a "107"!

"11" One-on-one isolation action (verbally cued as "ice"). This may occur inside (11 down) or outside (11 up). Isolation may be needed immediately (11 red), where the offensive player is isolated with the defensive player as soon as "red" is called. The isolation may be more effectively set up after several passes have occurred (11 blue). Teams that isolate well usually have practiced the isolations such that they do not interfere with the teams offensive rhythm. In order for one-on-one play to be most effective, all other players must understand why the isolation is to be used, their role within the design of the isolation, the purpose of the initial alignment, knowledge of the floor spacing, what to do if the isolation fails, and knowledge of key combination numbers which compliment the isolations:

1. Alignment is once again dependent on function. Who do we want to get open on the court and why? What do we want to take advantage of: our star player, or their

weak defensive player? A defensive player in foul trouble, sick, etc.? Where do we want our offensive player to receive the ball? When do we want him to be isolated (red - immediately, or blue - after several key passes)? And finally, how? The numbered motion offers the 6, 7, 8, or 9 method for effectively freeing an offensive man for the one-on-one game. The following combinations are suggested for this very purpose:

A. "9" - All stack action (9, 29, 39, 49) are excellent methods for freeing an offensive player for isolation.
  (1) 9, 11, or 2 (up or down, red or blue) single stack into the isolation for the 2 man.
  (2) 29, 11, or 2 (up or down, red or blue) double stack into the isolation for the 2 man.
  (3) 39, 11, or 2 (up or down, red or blue) triple stack into the isolation for the 2 man.
  (4) 49, 11, or 2 (up or down, red or blue) quadruple stack into the isolation for the 2 man.

B. "8" - All backdoor action which may include 6's and 7's initiated by a stack (9, 8, 11, 2) are excellent movements for isolating an offensive player.
  (1) 8, 11, 2 (up or down, red or blue) backdoor, isolates for the 2 man.
  (2) 9, 8, 11, 2 (up or down, red or blue) stack, then backdoor, isolates for the 2 man.
  (3) 8, 7, 11, 2 (up or down, red or blue) backdoor, pick and roll, isolates for the 2 man.
  (4) 8, 6, 11, 2 (up or down, red or blue) backdoor, screen down or up, isolates for the 2 man.

C. "7" - Pick and roll action, which may include 6's, 8's, or 9's is an excellent method for isolating various offensive players.
  [4](1) 11, 7, 2 (up or down, red or blue) isolation, pick and roll for 2.

---

[4] The sequence of numbers identifying the motion may begin with the isolation (11) instead of the 7 for variety and to discourage the opposition from "picking up the play." In function, "11, 7, 2" is the same as "7, 11, 2."

(2) 11, 742 (up or down, red or blue) isolation, pick and roll continuously with 4 and 2.

(3) 11, 29, 742 (up or down, red or blue) isolation, double stack, pick and roll continuously with 4 and 2.

(4) 11, 8, 72 (up or down, red or blue) isolation, backdoor, pick and roll for 2.

(5) 11, 6, 72 (up or down, red or blue) isolation, down or up screens, pick and roll for 2.

D. "6" - Screening up or down, "6 down" is a down pick, and "6 up" is a back pick, is another option. This may include combinations of 7, 8, 9 as described in the preceding paragraphs.

(1) 11, 6, 2 (up or down, red or blue) isolation, down or up pick for the 2 man.

(2) 11, 6, 72 (up or down, red or blue) isolation, down or up pick, pick and roll action for the 2 man.

As was described in the previous section, 742 would mean continuous pick and roll action for the 4 and 2 man.

(3) 11, 6, 82 (up or down, red or blue) isolation, down or up pick, back door action for the 2 man.

(4) 11, 6, 92 (up or down, red or blue) isolation, down or up pick, single stack action, for the 2 man.

2. Location of all players in relationship to their particular skill strength and coordinated with the movement of the isolated player is critical. Once the isolation occurs, all players must:

A. Continue motion with purpose, yet clear the operative isolation area.

B. Maintain intelligent spacing which permits teammates, other than the one isolated, to position themselves such that offensive skills may be best utilized once the offensive man begins his one-on-one move.

C. Ready themselves for action.
(1) Cut to the basket.
(2) Cut to a shallow shooting area.

(3) Cut to a deep shooting area.
(4) Pick for a teammate other than the isolated man.
(5) Pick for the isolated man.
(6) Receive a pass from the isolated man.
(7) Play two man games:
   (a) players not performing the isolation
   (b) players performing the isolation
(8) Gain inside rebounding position.
(9) Gain perimeter rebounding position.
(10) Quickly change from offense to defense.

One great advantage of the numbered motion offense is that it keeps the motion of the offense moving once the "isolation" is called. Therefore, if the isolation doesn't materialize, the team is not standing around wondering what may happen next. Movement is quickly continued by a number call.

"12" Horizontal or diagonal post picking (this may be from the low, mid, high, or short corner positions). Primary movement is to have the ballside player pick to the weakside of the court for the opposite man. "12R" reverses this picking order by having the weakside man pick the ballside post at any time.

1. Alignment is determined by personnel and function. Who, what, where, why, when, and how, will determine the most effective alignment to utilize the numbered motion strength and take advantage of specific weaknesses within the defense. Block-to-block power games low are effective against some defenses, while speed short corner, or high-low post action is more effective against others. Nevertheless, a wide range of post-to-post, post-to-forward, and post-to-guard number combinations may be created out of the 12 series.

    A. "9" - All stack action (9, 29, 39, 49) compliment the inside game options of 12.
       (1) 912 (low, mid, high, corner) single stack into a power post game inside.
       (2) 2912 (low, mid, high, corner) double stack into a power post game inside.
       (3) 3912 (low, mid, high, corner) triple stack into a power post game inside.
       (4) 4912 (low, mid, high, corner) quadruple stack into a power post game inside.

(5) 49125 (low, mid, high, corner) same as 4912, except that we are now going to the 5 man. This could also be called 9125 (single post stack), or just 125 (no stack). Weakside post guard pass 1250 (0) offers further counters to the weakside double down.

B. "8" - backdoor action is excellent for setting up the 12 power game.
  (1) 812 (low, mid, high, corner) wide spread into a power post game inside.
  (2) 9812 (low, mid, high, corner) single stack into a backdoor wide spread finishing with a power post game inside.
  (3) 98125 (low, mid, high, corner) single stack into a backdoor wide spread finishing with a power post game inside to the 5 man.

C. "7" or "70" is an integral part of the 12 series.
  (1) 712 (low, mid, high, corner) pick and roll into a power post game inside.
  (2) 9712 (low, mid, high, corner) pick and roll into a power post game inside.
  (3) 97125 (low, mid, high, corner) pick and roll into a power post game inside, keying continuous action with the 5 man.

D. "6" - Screening up or down, "6 down" is a down pick, and "6 up" is a back pick, is another option:
  (1) 612 (low, mid, high, corner) screens up and down into a power post game inside.
  (2) 9612 (low, mid, high, corner) single stack, screens up and down into a power post game inside.
  (3) 96125 (low, mid, high, corner) single stack, screens up and down into a power post game inside keying on the 5 man.

There are several other options with the 6 which are effective and should be mentioned in this section of the numbered function:
  (4) 126 (low, mid, high, corner) power post game inside with picking up or down (6).
  (5) 9126 (low, mid, high, corner) single stack, power post game inside finishing with picking up or down (6).
  (6) 91256 (low, mid, high, corner) single stack, power post game inside for the 5 man, finishing with picking up or down (6).

Obviously 12 has a myriad of options that cannot be presented in this text. However, the reader is encouraged to teach the "base" numbers to his team, and then build on this foundation as his personnel permits. We need always to be reminded that it is wise to do a few things well, rather than many things poorly.

"13" Any lob pass action. The lob may take place from the low, mid, high, short corner, or wing positions. Primary movement is to isolate any defensive player who is overplaying the post, wing, or guard and exploit the overplay with a lob pass resulting in a short jump shot or lay-up:

1. Alignment is determined by personnel and function. Who, what, where, why, when, and how will determine the most effective alignment to be used against the defense.

    A. "9" - All stack action (9, 29, 39, 49) are effective when setting up the lob (13).

    (1) 9135 (low, mid, high, corner, wing) single stack, lob to the 5 man. 4 or 5 indicate a post lob. Most post lobs are low, mid, high, or short corner, although there are times where 5 or 4 could be on the wing.

    (2) 9133 (low, mid, high, corner, wing) single stack, lob to the 3 man. Most lobs to 2 and 3 are from the wing. If the coach has a big point guard, or one with great athletic ability, he may receive the lob from the wing or cutting from the top of the key.

    (3) 29135 (low, mid, high, corner, wing) double stack, lob to the 5 man.

    (4) 39133 (low, mid, high, corner, wing) triple stack, lob to the 3 man.

    (5) 49133 (low, mid, high, corner, wing) quadruple stack, lob to the 3 man.

    B. "8" - Backdoor action is a great counter against pressure and increases the opportunity for the lob to be successful.

    (1) 8135 (low, mid, high, corner, wing) backdoor, lob to the 5 man.

    (2) 8133 (low, mid, high, corner, wing) backdoor, lob to the 3 man.

    (3) 8131 (low, mid, high, corner, wing) backdoor, lob to the 1 man.

    C. "7" or "70" may be used in the lob series.

    (1) "7" - However, if a pick and roll is called, the coach does not force the lob pass if a bounce or chest pass is easier to complete the play.

(2) "70" - Once again, the numbered play for a lob may be called, but a bounce or chest pass may be more efficient to complete the play.

D. "6" - Screening up or down offers great opportunities to lob the ball. If timed properly, the back screen lob play is one of the most popular plays (which often ends in a slam dunk) for the fans. Stacks may be used to initiate the offense, and a wide variety of combinations may follow:
(1) 6135 (low, mid, high, corner, wing) up or down pick, lob to the 5 man.
(2) 6133 (low, mid, high, corner, wing) up or down pick, lob to the 3 man.
(3) 6131 (low, mid, high, corner, wing) up or down pick, lob to the 1 man.

Usually the team with the greatest athletes is the team that continually uses the lob play. However, players who learn to read one another's cuts and perfect the coordination between the lob and the quick break to the basket, are the players who will use the lob effectively.

"14" Snapback action. The ballhandler on top draws the defense with him, then snaps the ball back to the opposite wing for a shot or a post feed. The snapback may be used from 6, 7, 8, or 9 motion numbers and will be discussed in detail later in the text.

"15" Drive draw and kick action. Once again, this offensive action may occur after any of the motion numbers have been put into play. However, the fundamental skill involved in 15 is to have a penetrator draw two defensive men on him, while the man who is open moves to an open area to receive the ball. Simply by calling 15 is a great verbal cue for this fundamental action - driving to the basket and hitting the open man once the double team occurs.

"16" Perimeter weak or strongside blind pick action. Weak or strongside blind pick action is primarily used as a "crutch" play series. The uniqueness to 16's action is that most offensive perimeter picks on the weak or strongside are front picks (which include "slip" cuts and step out movements of the picker). The back pick's primary function is to free the perimeter player for the jump shot, and secondary action is to look for the screener who is slashing to the basket or popping for the short jump shot. This is a continuous perimeter back pick action that will be discussed in detail later in the text.

"17"   Any combination or 7, 70, or 6 action where 7 or 70 is followed by a 6. It is a pick the picker option. This is a "crutch" play that will be discussed in a later chapter.

"18"   Any combination of 12 and 6 action where a 12 is followed by a 6. This is another "crutch" play that will be described in detail later in the text.

On first examination, functions of the numbered motion offense seem overwhelming. The options appear endless and the combinations too innumerable for any team to comprehend. However, let the coach be reminded of the astronomer who after the first time he looked at the midnight skies was bewildered because he saw only a myriad of disconnected stars. But, after diligent study of the solar systems and constellation patterns, simple configurations began to give the heavens order. This is the nature of the numbered motion offense; when the numbers' designs are comprehended, form and function readily follow. Be patient while you study the combinations. Once they are understood, the reader, like the astronomer, will be amazed at the system's simplicity.

Chapter 5

Teaching the Numbered Motion Offense

Chapter 5
Teaching the Numbered Motion Offense

As was described in the forward of this book, the reader should have a grasp of the basic motion offense and its functions before attempting to understand how the numbered motion offense should be taught. It is not the purpose of the text to articulate to the reader the essentials of the motion game, but to build on those essentials an effective offensive system that offers greater control of the offense's primary movements by the players and coach. Therefore, Chapter 5 will deal with five areas which will enhance the effectiveness of teaching and applying the numbered motion offensive system. These five areas are: selling the offense, teaching the "whole" concept of the offense, teaching the "parts" concept of the offense, combining the "whole" with its "parts," and applying the offense to game situations.

Selling the offense.

My dad was a musician and often would remark, "You may have the greatest song in the world, but if the studio will not record it, you will take it with you to your grave." Convincing oneself, then convincing the players that the numbered motion offense will improve their individual and team skills while increasing their opportunity to be successful is the most critical phase in developing the offense:

First and foremost, the coach must believe in the offense. Before the coach can teach the players to believe in the offense, he must believe in it himself. Therefore he must do the following:

1. Gain all the knowledge available on the subject: books, tapes, game films, magazine articles, etc. Devour the present material such that you may become an authority on the strengths and weaknesses of the numbered motion game. If for some reason the coach doesn't institute the offensive system within his own game, then at the very worst, he has increased his knowledge as to how to counter such a system once his team faces it.

2. Be able to articulate clearly to the team that the motion numbered game is not as complicated as it first appears. It is a system which simply puts numbers on fundamental skills and permits us to apply those numbers to game situations.

Then the players must believe in the offense. There are several ways to develop this belief:

1. "Chalk talks" never take the place of on the floor action, but this will give the players the big picture of the numbered motion game. Let them:
   (a) see their roles in the offense,
   (b) see what fundamental skills they need to work on within the offense,
   (c) gain an understanding of the base numbers and how the system is built on the present offense,
   (d) understand how the numbers improve communication between the team members and the coach,
   (e) offer suggestions - some of the most effective number combinations come from the players,
   (f) ask questions of any phase they don't understand regarding the offense.

2. Outside sources are important; the numbered motion offense is relatively new to the college game. Videos, magazines, and training films by successful professional teams using the system will help to convince players of the viability of the offense.

3. In this instance, the coach does not need to be a salesman, but a teacher; "the product sells itself." If the coach understands how the numbers assist his present offense, is able to clearly teach the players how to apply these numbers to their basic fundamental development, and assist them in more efficient team functioning, then the players will eagerly embrace the offense.

Teaching the "whole" of the numbered motion offense.

When presenting a concept that is innovative, such as the numbered motion offense, caution must be balanced between the mind-set of being "under-whelmed," or "over-whelmed" by a new idea, and focusing the student on basic principles:

1. "Under-whelmed" - from the beginning, insist that the players realize that this is not a secret stealth bomber attack weapon. The offense will not <u>work</u> unless they do. All aspects of an effective offensive system must strive for perfect execution in order for the offense to reach its most efficient potential.

2. "Over-whelmed" - secondly, it is easy to become overwhelmed by the number of combinations which exist within the offense. However, as the coach explains how the numbers apply to the game of basketball, players will realize that the numbers are simply describing what they are presently doing. The numbers aids the team to perform in a more coordinated fashion by helping them communicate more effectively with one another. The numbers are to be used to clarify basic function, not to confuse it! Therefore, in presenting the whole, give the players the basic numbers 6 through 13:

"6"   Screening up or down; 6 up is a backpick and 6 down is a frontpick.

"7"   Pick and roll action.

"70"   Pick and roll play where the big man handles the ball and hands off to the small man. The main actions are "big on little" or "little on big."

"8"   Backdoors, early release on a pick/roll, (7 or 70) plus 6's or 12's. Secondly, "8" may be called for a backdoor open cut series if the defensive pressure is fully extended. "8" also creates many give and go situations because of the extended defense.

"9"   Stack action involving 2,3, or 4 offensive players. Stack action may include curls, "pop in," "pop out," pick the picker, etc.

"10"   Curls - On any elbow, or at a middle or low post downpick, the offensive team may use the curl option. The man who sets the downpick will pop back as the low man curls. Use the principle "little" picking for "big" or "big" picking for "little" in this game action.

"11"   One-on-one isolation action.

"12"   Horizontal or diagonal post picking (this may be from the low, mid, high, or short corner positions). Primary movement is to have the ballside player pick to the weakside of the court for the opposite man. "12R" reverses this picking order by having the weakside man pick the ballside post at any time.

"13"   Any lob pass action.

Next, ask the players if there is some phase of basketball that they have never seen which appears in the numbers 6 through 13. They will obviously answer, "NO!" This will help clarify the simplicity of the numbers in the players' minds. Then ask if there is any confusion regarding the understanding of the base numbers.

Then ask the players what skill aspects of the offense would be important regarding their position (guard, forward, or center) in the execution of the various numbers. Talk them slowly through each number to ensure clarity of position responsibility.

Now break the team into position groups and let them discuss each number, their role, and how the player's individual skills fit with the "whole" of that number. Emphasis during this teaching phase is to have the student understand the whole as it relates to the part, and not vice versa. Later, when we discuss how the part is related to the whole, the emphasis will change to the part rather than the whole.

After the players are comfortable with their role in relating to the offensive scheme's number, return to the original team meeting posture and explain to the team how the numbers may be interwoven within the system. The author would suggest leading the discussion with the following thought sequence to show how the "whole" of the numbered motion combinations complement the basic motion offense:

<u>6 series</u> - building the 6 series:

(1) "Can we begin the 6 series with a stack offense? How? 96. What does the floor alignment look like? Where are you? Why? What is your primary function in 96? What happens if someone forgets to stack? Can we continue the motion with 6 action even though the 9 was not set?"

(2) "Can we begin the 6 series with a double stack offense? How? With two 9's. Is that 699, 996, or 296? Generally speaking, 699 is not the best verbal cue because we do not want to begin an offense with up and down screens, then regress to a static double stack. 996 is fine, but it conflicts with the total number system, as we will see later. Therefore, 296 communicates clearly that we want a double stack, then follow with a 6 series up and down pick action." It is imperative that the coach leads the discussion rather than open up a "Pandora's Box" of every creative method that

could come up to describe how to communicate the double stack option that finishes with up and down screens. The initial meeting is also not the time to add alignment, location, time and score, or other game parameters. Remember the intent is to give the players an overview of what the numbers represent and how they may be used in game situations to assist the coach and player in executing a particular fundamental aspect of the game.

(3) By now, one of the players has thought of a triple stack leading into a 6 action game (396). If the quadruple stack (496) is suggested, the teacher-coach knows it's time to move on to the next concept.

(4) If one player is "hot," is it possible to focus on feeding him the ball using the numbered motion offense? Yes. We may want to continue the action of the stack (9) and the down and up screens (6) to free the player. Other than your name, how are you identified in the offensive system? By position - guard, forward, center; and those positions have numbers. The 1 guard, 2 guard, 3 forward, 4 forward, and 5 center have defined roles. How may we identify the method and the player we want to get open? The method, stack (9) with down and up screens (6), we have already identified; now we must identify the player. Let us attempt to get 2 open. To communicate "freeing 2" to every team member on the court, we may call "962." This lets everyone know what we want to do and how we want to do it." Once again, alignment and floor placement of players should not be discussed at this time. However, this is an excellent opportunity to discuss shot selection and continue to define the players' offensive roles. The question will or must be asked, "Coach, if we call 962 and I'm not the 2 man, do I shoot the ball if I'm wide open?" "Only if it's a <u>high</u> percentage shot! A high percentage shot is generally defined as a shot you can make 75% of the time. A "good" percentage shot is a shot that you can make at least 50% of the time. So if your number is <u>not</u> called, and you are left wide open by the defensive team, you know whether or not to take the shot based on your shooting ability and offensive role." This is also a good time to discuss other factors that are always important in shot selection: time, score, tempo of the game, etc.

The teacher-coach should continue taking his team through the numbers of the motion offense, making sure the team understands the "whole" before becoming involved in the "parts."

Chapter Four's detailed description of the numbered motion's functions and options will be of assistance to the coach as he presents the "whole" of the offense to his team.

Teaching the "parts" of the numbered motion offense.

If the teacher-coach does not know the basic fundamentals that need to be taught in the game of basketball, it will be very difficult to add numbers to a "dysfunctional" skill level team and expect a high level of performance. Let's look first at the fundamental skills that need to be developed by centers, guards, and forwards.

In *Progressions For Teaching Basketball* by Mel Hankinson, each player position is identified, then a progression for teaching that skill follows. The "parts" begin with the stationary location of each player position; then the interaction between centers, guards, and forwards are articulated. (Page 49 identifies the specific "parts" of the position breakdown and skill responsibilities and includes a "Key to Diagrams." The succeeding pages describe progressive steps in teaching each skill - Drill Teaching Progressions.)

Please turn to the next page to see how these parts are identified. The center's action is found on pages 50-57; then the guard's play on 57-58, and the forward's fundamental skills are progressively taught on pages 58-60.

When teaching, there is always a tension between the "part" and the "whole." The most effective teacher understands that repetition with intensity and enthusiasm is necessary in both areas while trying to balance the needs of an offensive system. However, the master teacher perfects the "part" which makes an efficient functioning "whole."

Position Break Down and Skill Responsibilities

CENTERS: 43
1. Getting open - emphasis on footwork. 43
2. Passing from the post. 44
3. Feeding from the post. 45
4. Basic offensive moves and shots. 45
5. Various turns. 47
6. Various shots. 48
7. Screening - weak side and strong side. 48
8. Getting rebounding position and tipping. 49

GUARDS: 50
1. Passing to the center and cutting. 50
2. Passing to the wing and cutting. 50
3. Passing to the wing and reversing. 50
4. Setting screens for wing men or guards. 51
5. Guard forward series. 51
6. Work on dribble drives ending with a shot, pivot, or pass. 51

FORWARDS: 51
1. Getting open - emphasis on footwork. 52
2. Passing to the center and cutting. 52
3. Driving off the set screen by guard for the shot or pass. 52
4. Reverse drive and straight shot. 52
5. Reversing without ball. 52
6. Getting open to receive the pass on the side post and from the weak side. 52
7. Offensive moves on the side post. 53
8. Screening for the guard. 53
9. Keeping the defensive man busy. 53
10. Getting the rebounding position. 53

Key to Diagrams

Cut - the straight line shows the movement of the offensive or defensive player (   ).
Dribble - usually indicated by a zig-zag line; an arrow at the end of the line indicates the direction of the dribble (   ).
Movement - from one area to the other (   ).
Pass - shown by a dotted line; an arrow at the end of the line shows the direction of the pass (   ).
Pivot or Roll - by the offensive or defensive player (   ).
Possession - the numbered player circled indicates possession of the ball (   ).
Return Pass - (2   1) 2 passes to 1 and 1 returns the ball to 2.
Screen - by an offensive player (   ).
Various Options of the Offensive Player - (   ) cut, pass, or dribble.

Centers: 1. Getting Open: A. Straight Break (Footwork)

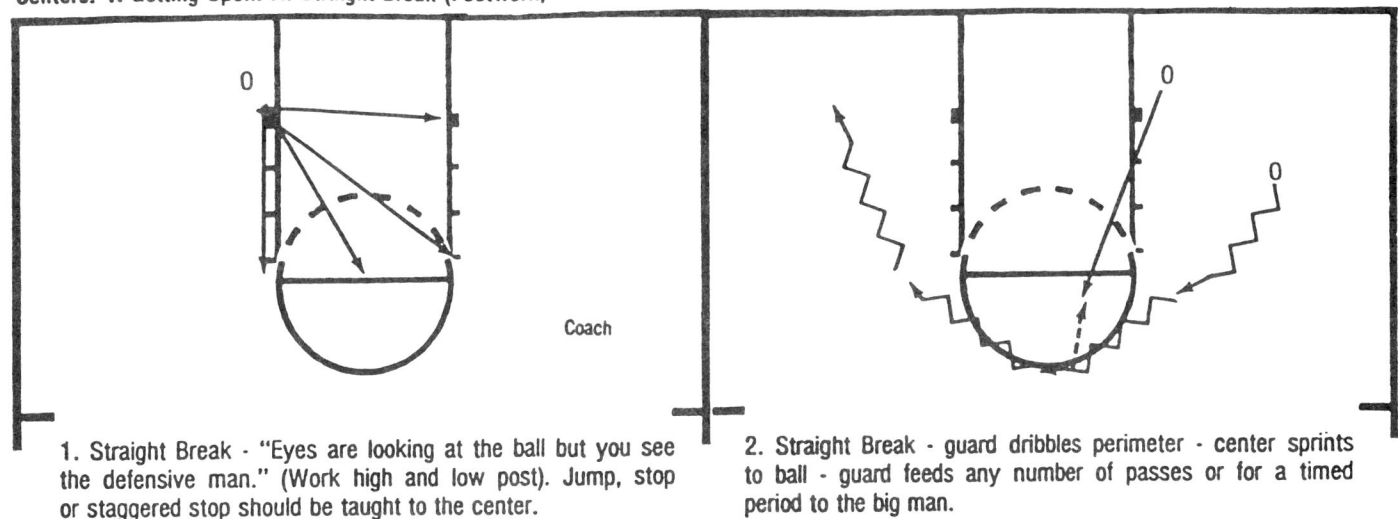

1. Straight Break - "Eyes are looking at the ball but you see the defensive man." (Work high and low post). Jump, stop or staggered stop should be taught to the center.

2. Straight Break - guard dribbles perimeter - center sprints to ball - guard feeds any number of passes or for a timed period to the big man.

Centers: B. Fake left go right or vice versa   Centers: C. Fake left go left or vice versa   Same drills

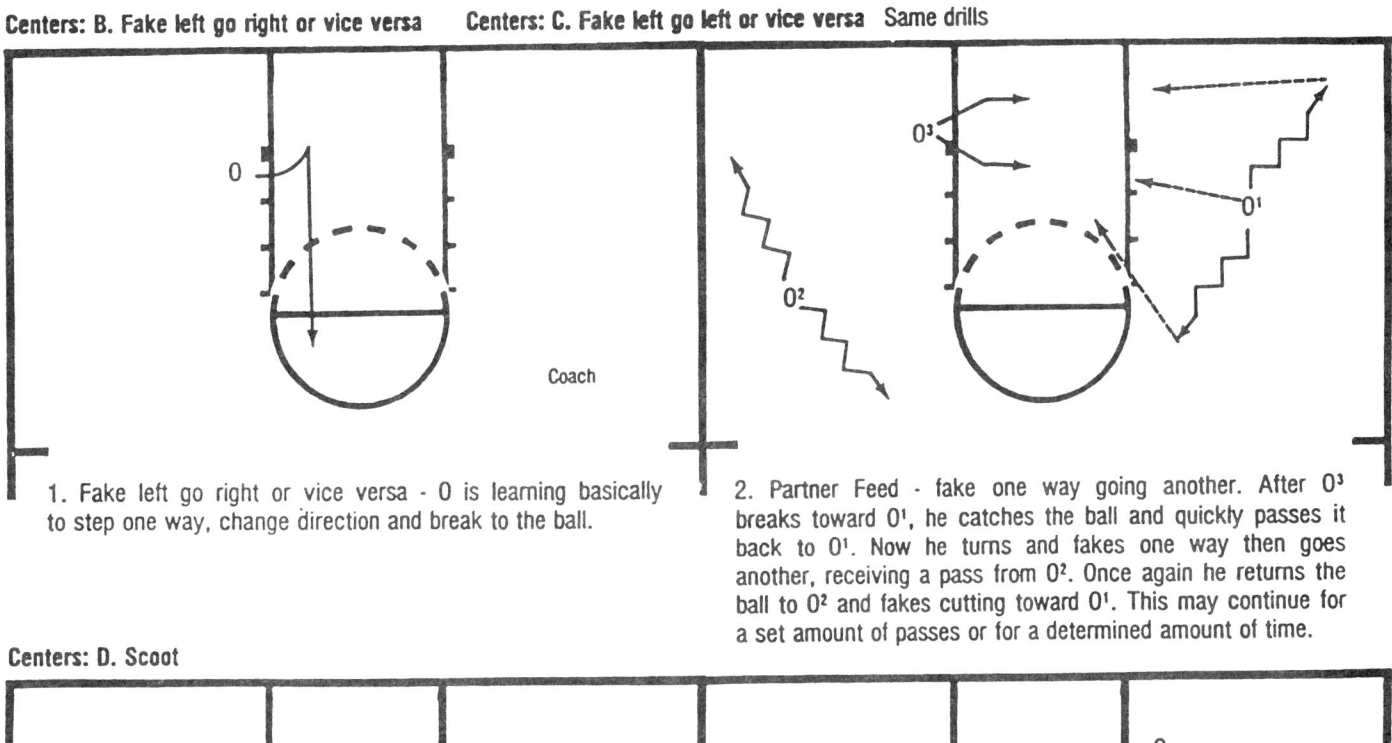

1. Fake left go right or vice versa - O is learning basically to step one way, change direction and break to the ball.

2. Partner Feed - fake one way going another. After O³ breaks toward O¹, he catches the ball and quickly passes it back to O¹. Now he turns and fakes one way then goes another, receiving a pass from O². Once again he returns the ball to O² and fakes cutting toward O¹. This may continue for a set amount of passes or for a determined amount of time.

Centers: D. Scoot

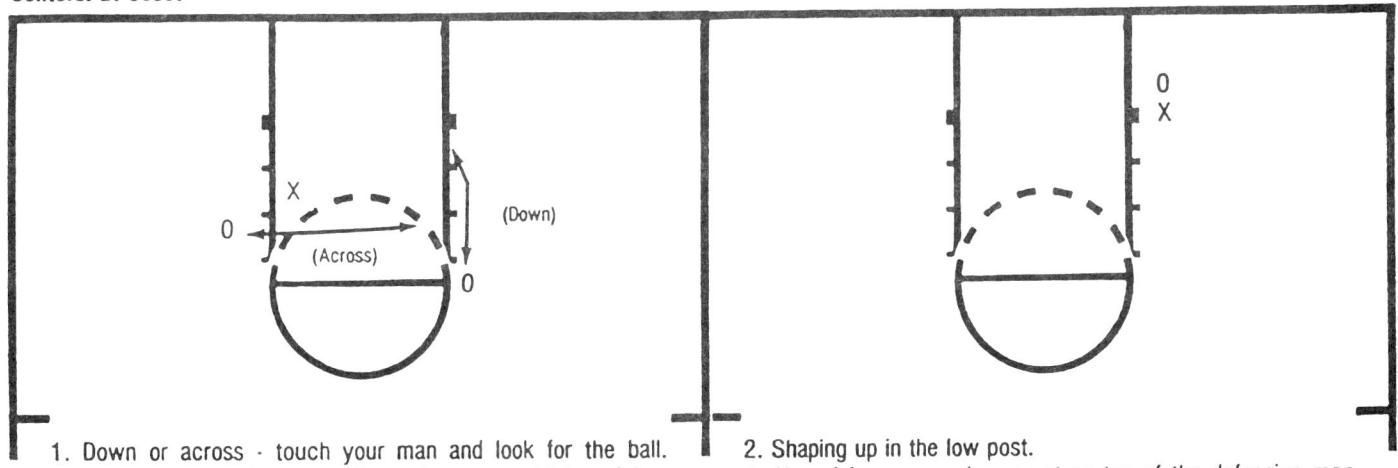

1. Down or across - touch your man and look for the ball. After O learns the footwork of scooting across high and low then the coach should add a "dummy" defensive player. Now O learns to "feel" where the defensive man is who is guarding him.

2. Shaping up in the low post.
A. Use of forearms - always get on top of the defensive man and spread those elbows wide.
B. Stick your butt drill - into the defensive man and call for the ball.

43

Centers: E. Step Away

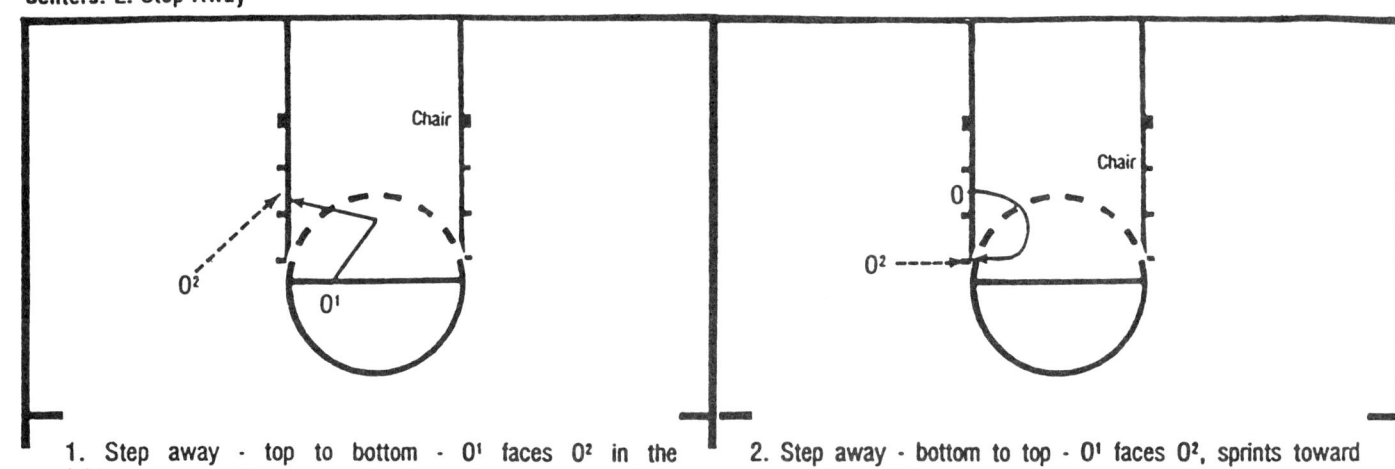

1. Step away - top to bottom - O¹ faces O² in the initial phase of the move. He then steps away as if he were going to set a pick on the chair located on the weakside low post area. After taking a few steps, he turns and cuts back to the strongside of the court in the low post area.

2. Step away - bottom to top - O¹ faces O², sprints toward the chair as if he were going to set a pick on the chair, then turns and pops high to receive the pass from O².

Centers: F. Reverse Pivot

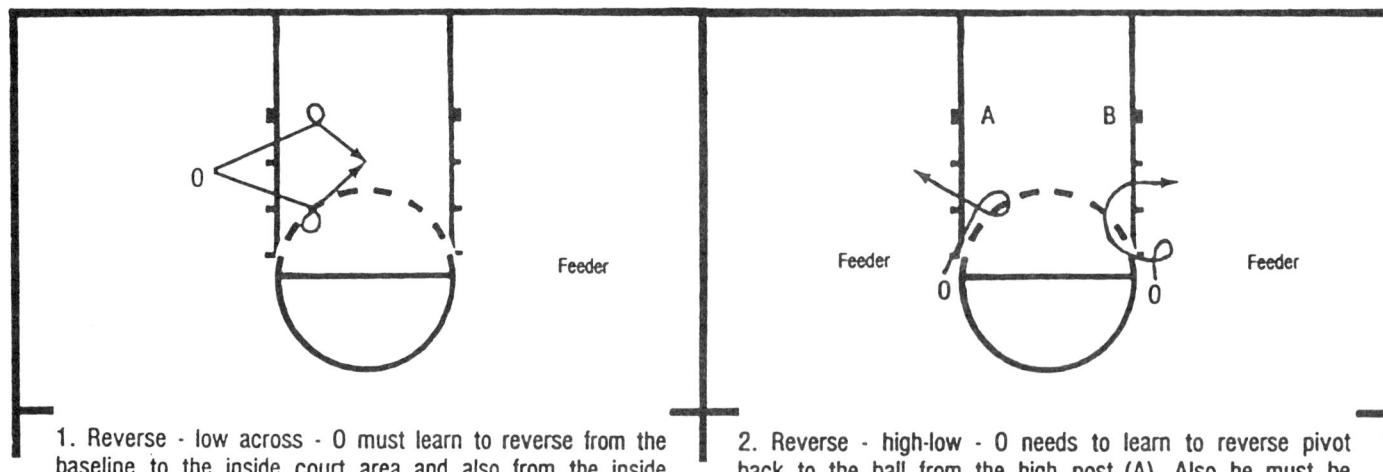

1. Reverse - low across - O must learn to reverse from the baseline to the inside court area and also from the inside court area to the baseline. Later add a "feeder" to pass O the ball only after he has properly executed the reverse pivot.

2. Reverse - high-low - O needs to learn to reverse pivot back to the ball from the high post (A). Also he must be taught the quick reverse pivot away from the ball (this is necessary because the defensive player may play him such that he will not let O slide directly to the low post). This is shown in B's position in the above diagram.

Centers: 2. Passing From Post (Low Post - High Post) A. Give and Go

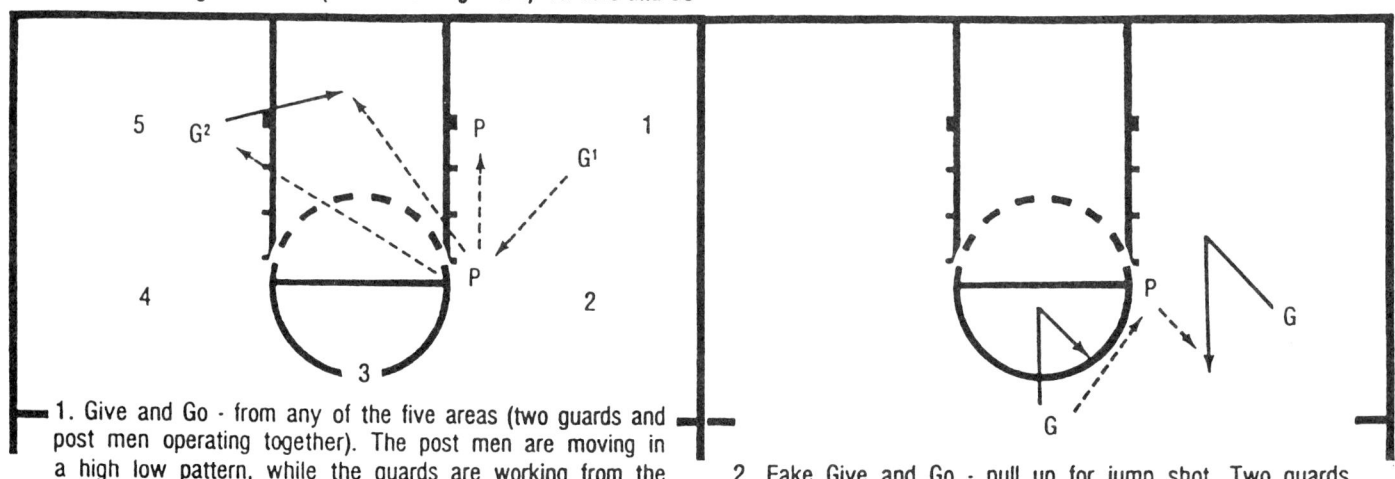

1. Give and Go - from any of the five areas (two guards and post men operating together). The post men are moving in a high low pattern, while the guards are working from the perimeter. Once the ball is passed into the post areas, the guard makes his cut to the hoop. The post man has the option of returning the pass to the person who threw him the ball, passing to the other post men or releasing the ball back outside.

2. Fake Give and Go - pull up for jump shot. Two guards are working the perimeter areas with one post man. The post player may cut high, low or operate from a medium post. Once the ball is passed into the post, the guards fake a sharp backdoor cut, then "V" cut back out and receive the ball from the post man for a jump shot.

Centers: A. Give and Go (Cont.)

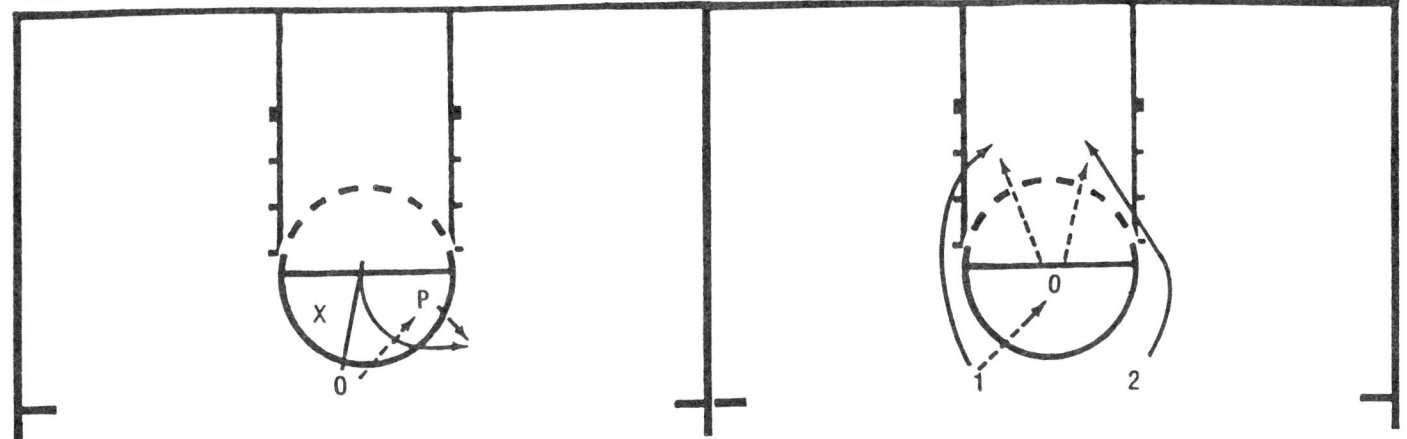

3. Fake Give and Go and come behind for jump shot or drive - post man tries to hang defense on his back. He must be taught how to pivot into the defensive player in order to free the offensive man for the shot.

4. Give and Go or fake give and go for jump shot. On this drill use two balls - post must react to all his players. The post player may work high or low but now he fakes the give and go every other pass and takes the jump shot.

Centers: 3. Feeding From Post (Low Post - High Post) A. Weakside Feeds

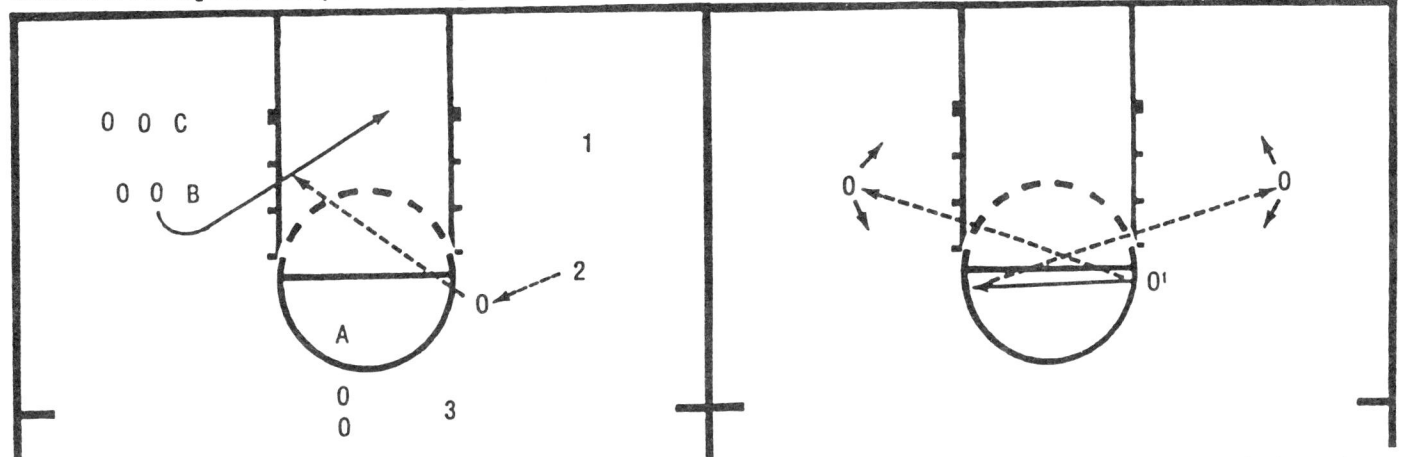

1. Weakside feeds - the center receives passes from 1, 2, 3 areas and hits cutters from areas A, B and C. He may work high or low in this drill series. After six passes, another post men steps in.

2. Deep weakside feeds - it is necessary to teach the post man how to look across zones and feed the forward or guard who is sliding to the weakside corners. After six passes, a new post man takes O¹'s spot.

Centers: 4 Offensive Moves A. Catch and Go - Take It In His Face

1. Jump stop - every night forwards and centers should catch at least one pass and come to a jump stop from each of these areas.

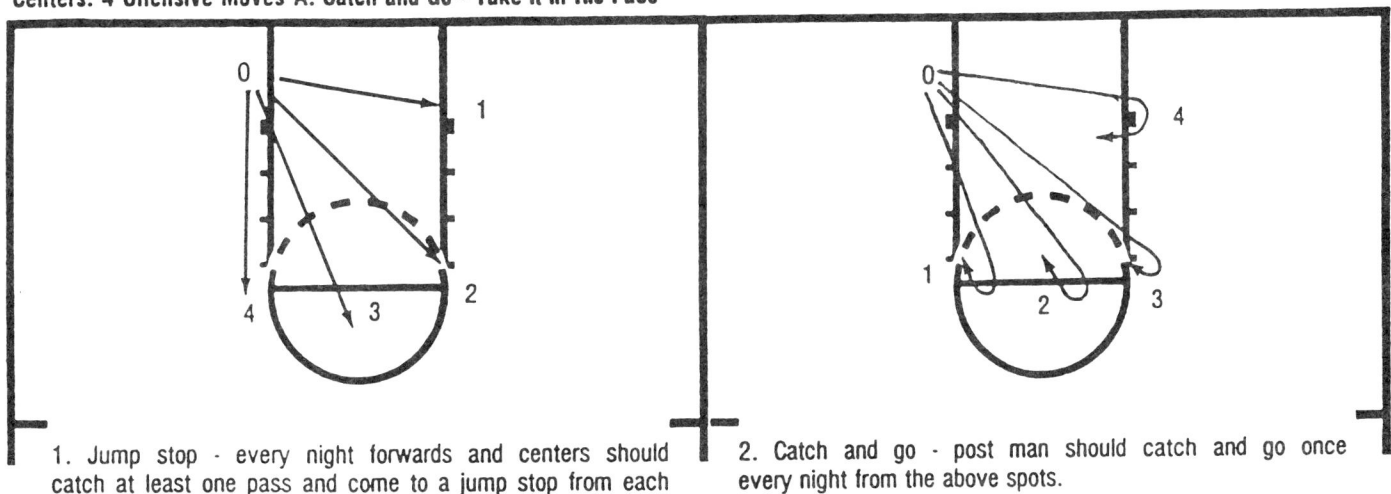

2. Catch and go - post man should catch and go once every night from the above spots.

45

Centers: 4 Offensive Moves A. Catch and Go - Take It In His Face (Cont.)

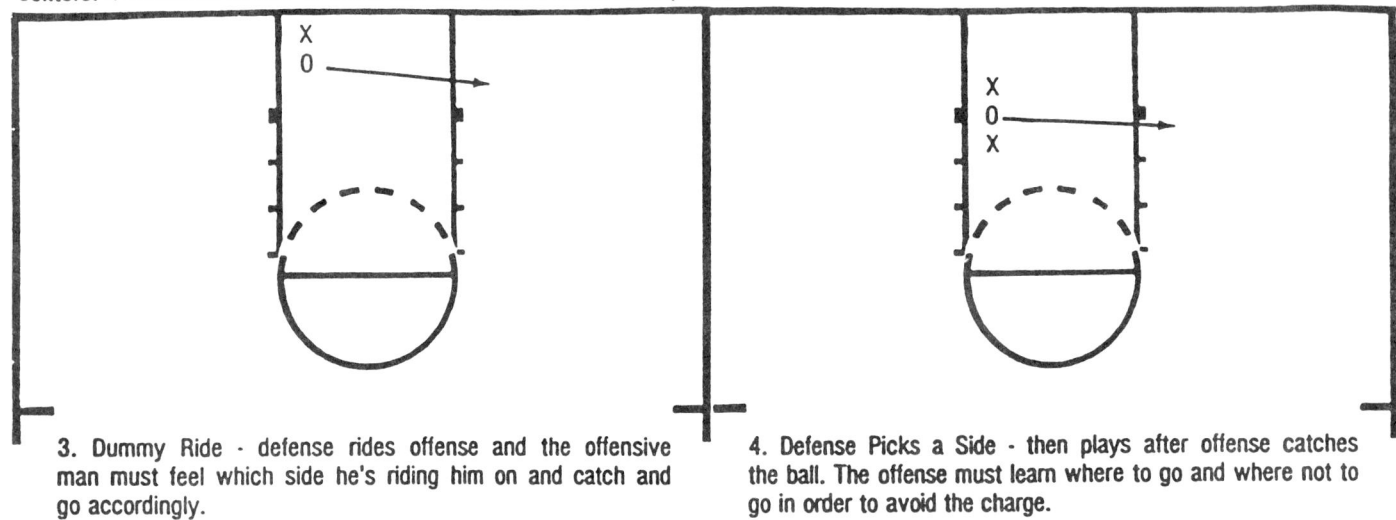

3. Dummy Ride - defense rides offense and the offensive man must feel which side he's riding him on and catch and go accordingly.

4. Defense Picks a Side - then plays after offense catches the ball. The offense must learn where to go and where not to go in order to avoid the charge.

Centers: B. Show The Ball Go Opposite - Take It In his Face

1. Show the ball go opposite - same defensive-offensive sequence as A.

Centers: C. Show The Ball Go Same Way

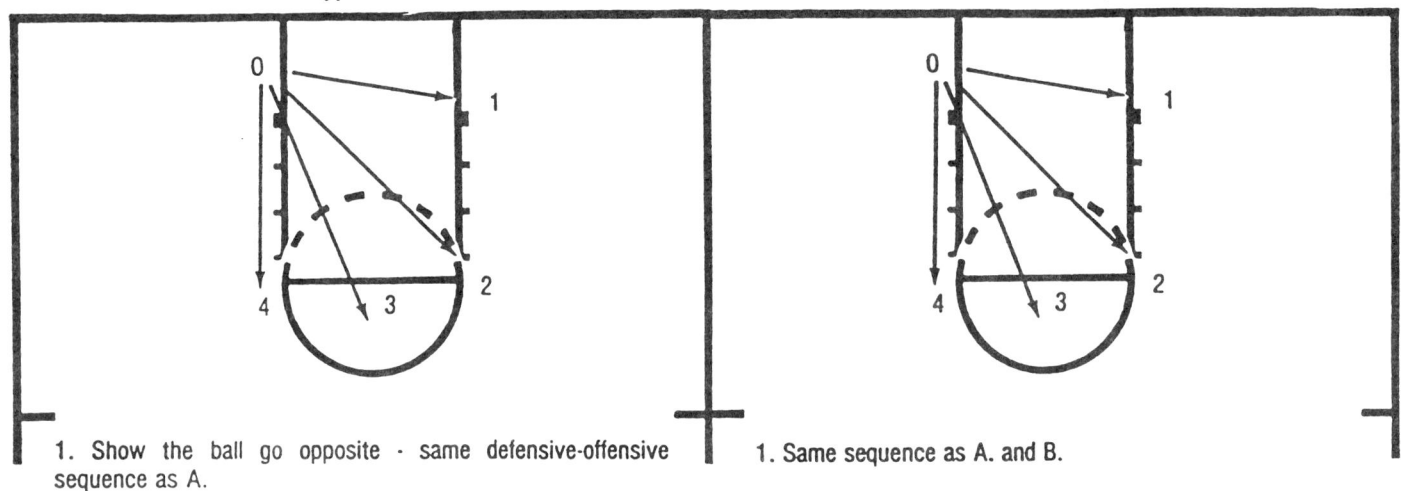

1. Same sequence as A. and B.

Centers: D. Drop Step and Go

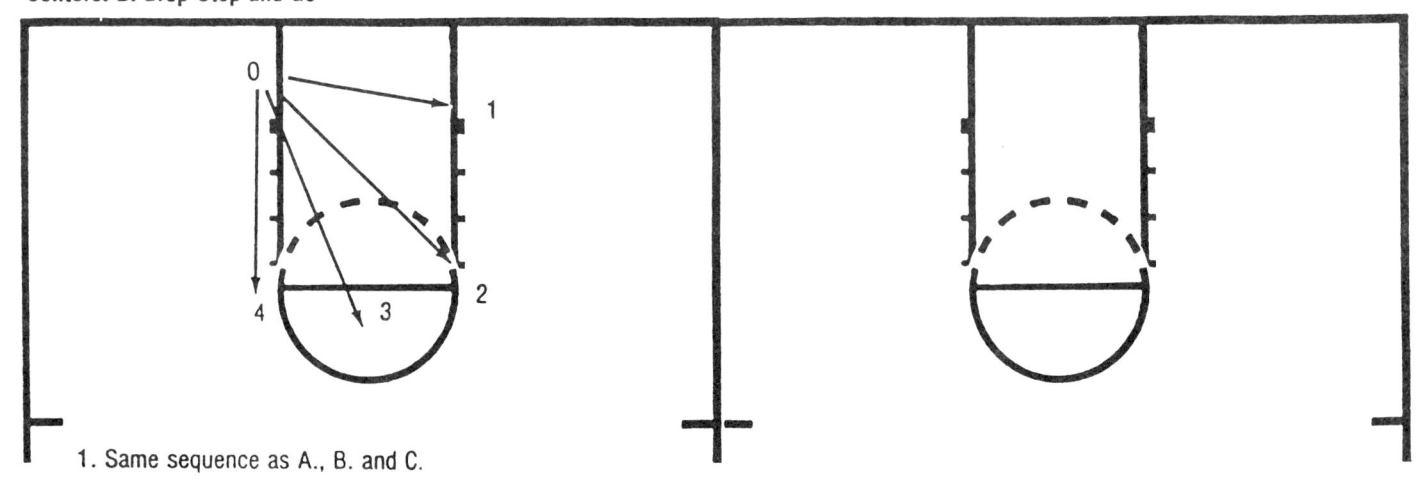

1. Same sequence as A., B. and C.

46

Centers: E. Pivot Face the Basket

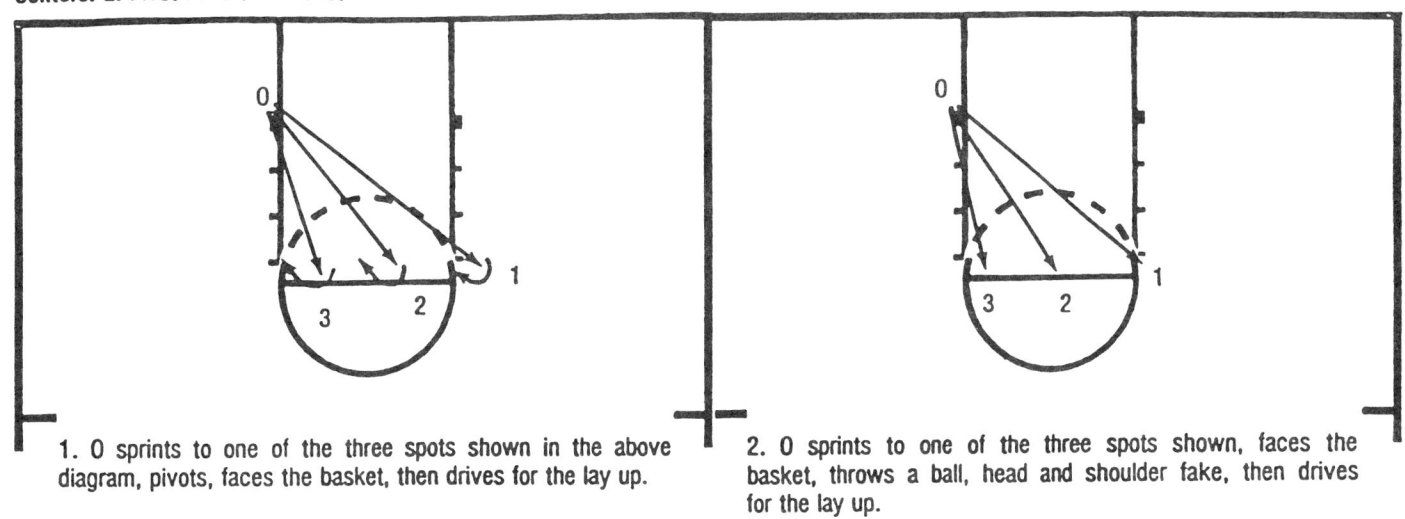

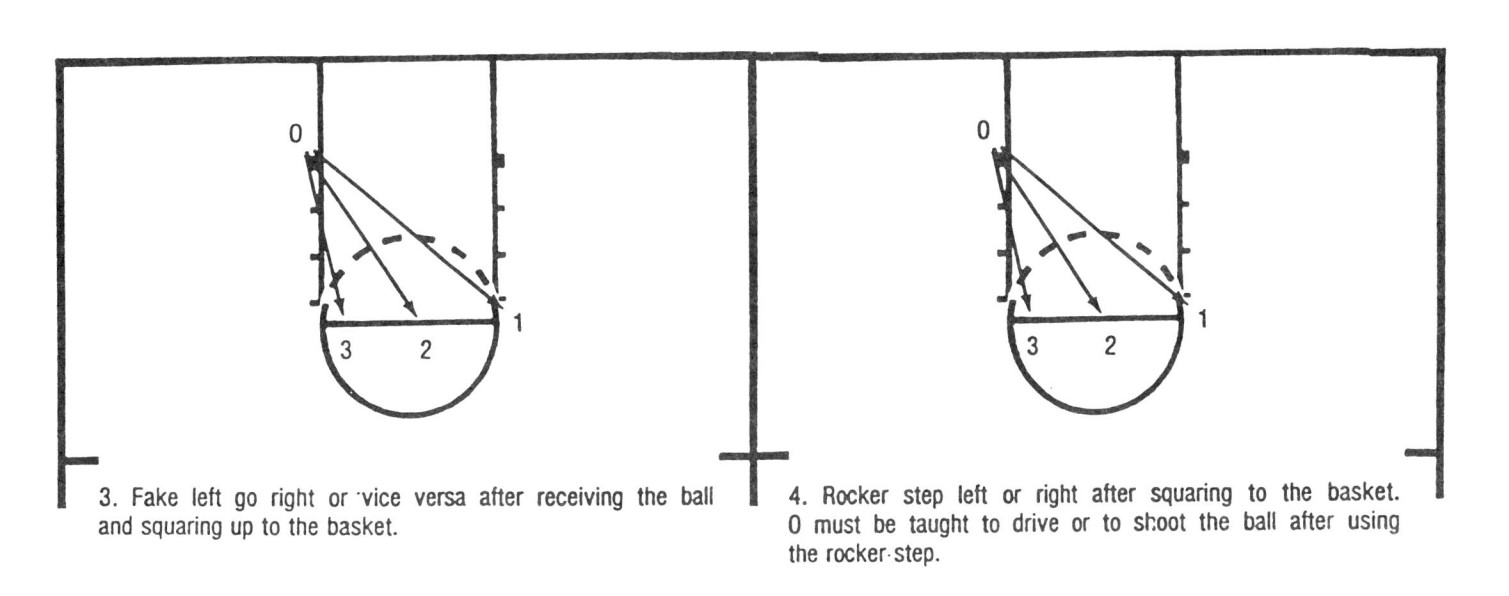

1. O sprints to one of the three spots shown in the above diagram, pivots, faces the basket, then drives for the lay up.

2. O sprints to one of the three spots shown, faces the basket, throws a ball, head and shoulder fake, then drives for the lay up.

3. Fake left go right or vice versa after receiving the ball and squaring up to the basket.

4. Rocker step left or right after squaring to the basket. O must be taught to drive or to shoot the ball after using the rocker-step.

Centers: 5. Various Turns (Offensive Moves)

1. Sprint Jump Stop:
   A. Outside turn
   B. Inside turn
   C. Outside Pivot
   D. Inside Pivot
All of these skills must be perfected by the post player.

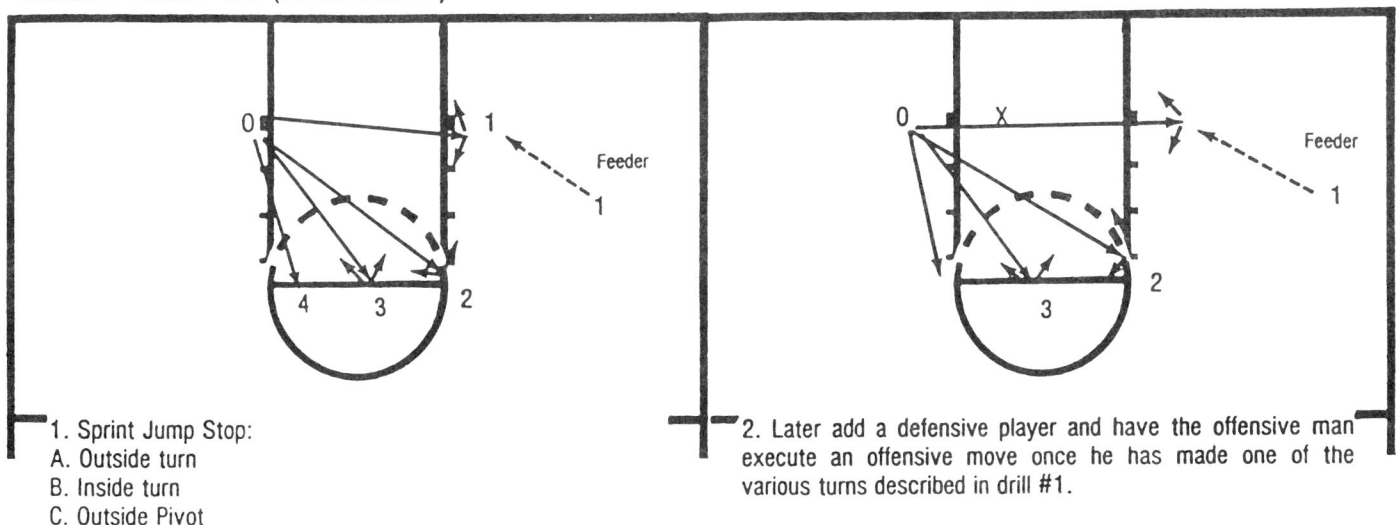

2. Later add a defensive player and have the offensive man execute an offensive move once he has made one of the various turns described in drill #1.

Centers: 6. Various Shots

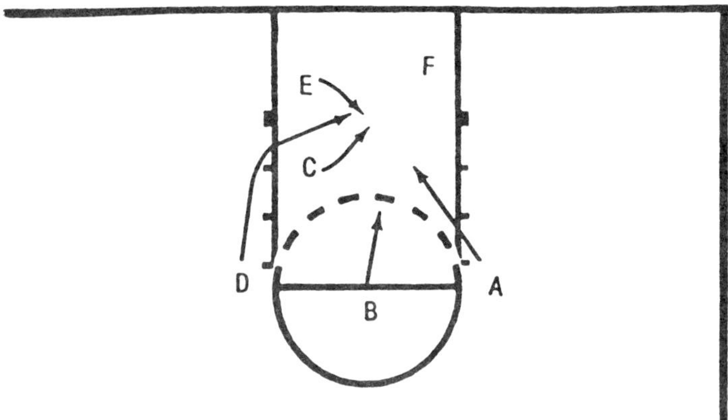

1. These shots need to be perfected by the post player:
   A. Right and left handed
   B. Right and left cross over
   C. Right and left reverse
   D. Right and left opposite hand underhand lay up
   E. Right and left lay back
   F. Right and left back out

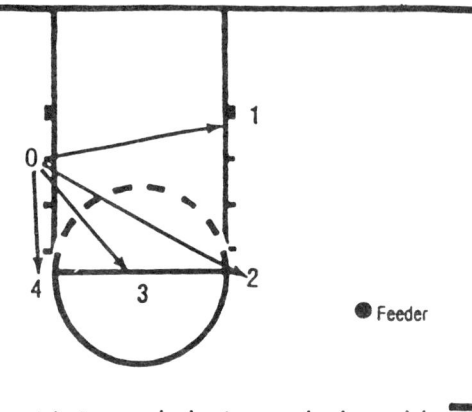

2. Jump shot - catch turn and shoot - emphasize gaining body balance after catching the ball properly; squaring the players shoulders to the basket; going straight up for the shot.

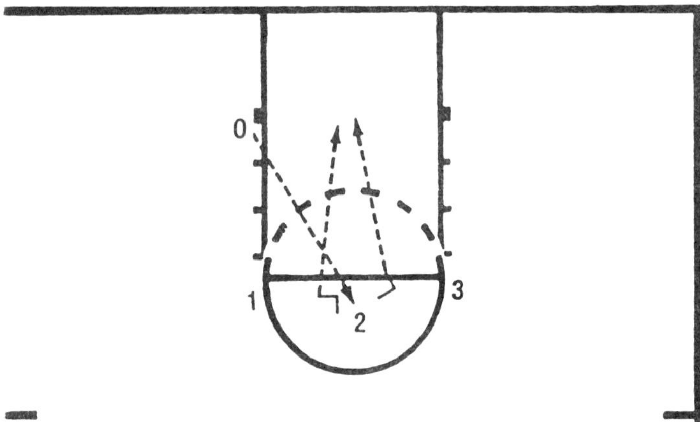

3. Jump Shot - one bounce shot - emphasize the same skills as in drill two, but now pay more attention to the **power dribble** (do not let the post man take a dead bounce before he shoots the ball, but insist on a quick explosive dribble that gives the offensive player a type of movement which will free him from the defensive player).

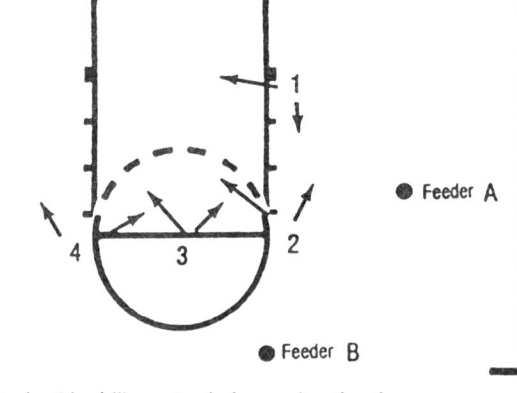

4. Jump shot - In this drill emphasis is on shooting from:
   A. Stationary position - the post man makes two jump shots from each of the four positions above.
   B. Cutting position - the feeder now moves to the wings, and the post man cuts from the four positions shown above making two shots from each position.

Centers: 7. Screening - Weakside and Strongside

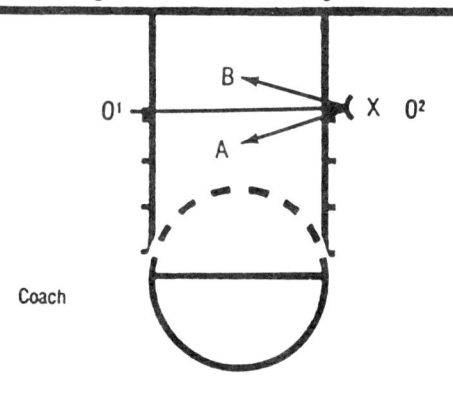

1. Weakside: Low - go get the man - O¹ must learn to:
   A. Come back high
   B. Come back low
   If he cuts properly then the coach throws him the ball for the lay up.

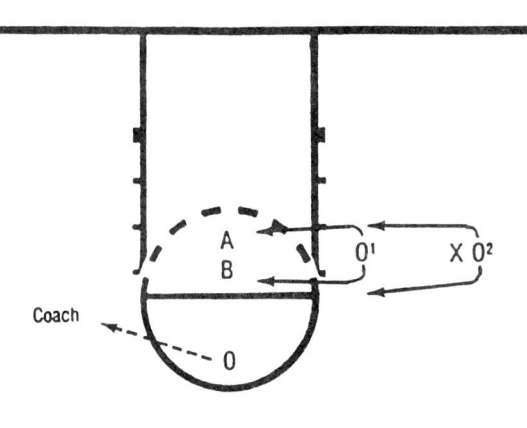

2. Weakside: Low - rub screen - O¹ must learn how to move once O² goes by:
   A. Come back high
   B. Come back low
   Later add a second defensive player on O¹ and play for real.

48

Centers: 7. Screening - Weakside and Strongside (Cont.)

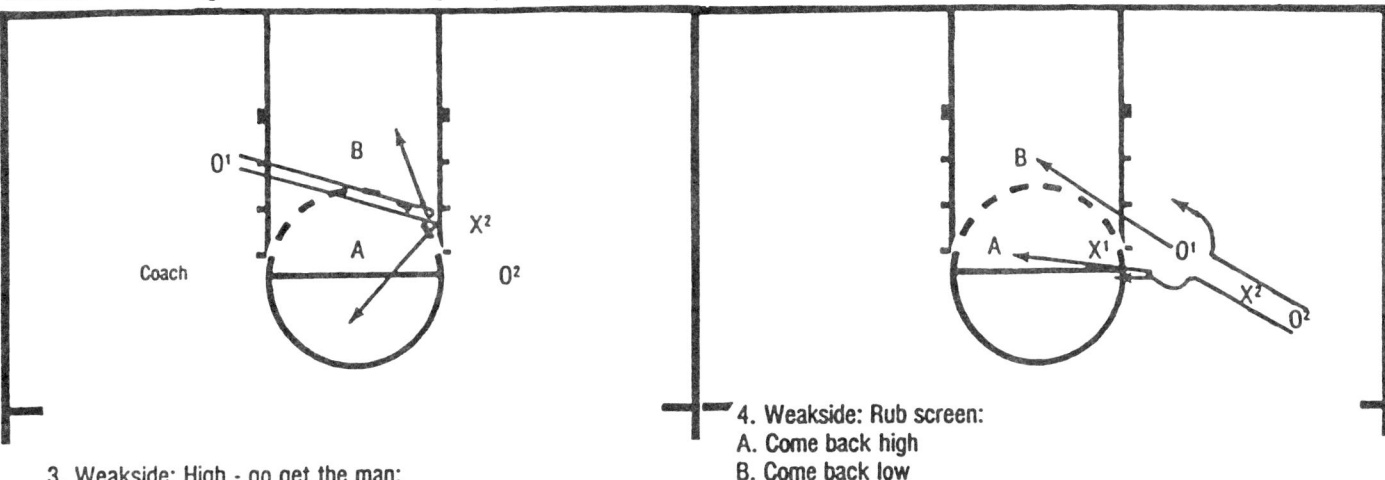

3. Weakside: High - go get the man:
A. Come back high
B. Come back low
It is important that O^1 learns to stop just before reaching X^2 so he does not illegally slam into him.

4. Weakside: Rub screen:
A. Come back high
B. Come back low
Teach O^1 to read whether or not X^1 has switched on O^2. If X^1 switches on O^2, then O^1 should immediately break to the basket. O^1 must also be taught how to keep X^2 on "his back" as he breaks high or low to receive the ball.

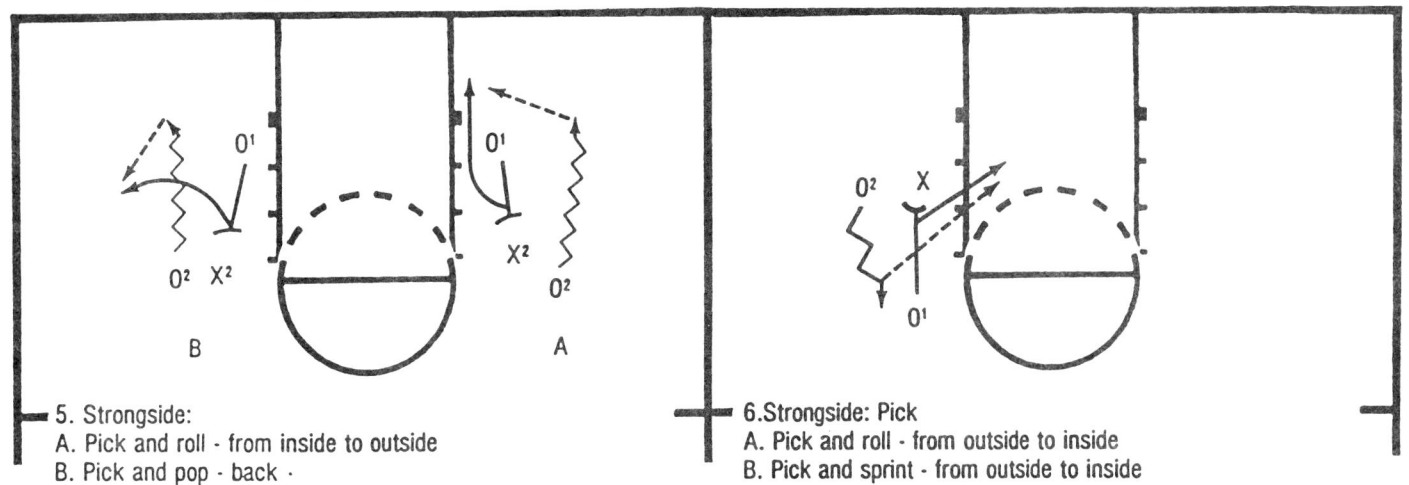

5. Strongside:
A. Pick and roll - from inside to outside
B. Pick and pop - back
Emphasis on the pick and roll is body position. O^1 must be taught to keep X^2 on his back so that he is free for the lay-up. On the pop back, O^1 must see if the defensive player is cheating low. If he is, then O^1 should pop out for the jump shot.

6. Strongside: Pick
A. Pick and roll - from outside to inside
B. Pick and sprint - from outside to inside
Emphasis on the pick and roll should be the same as mentioned in diagram 5. But the pick and sprint should be executed like a brush block in football as O^1 cuts to the basket.

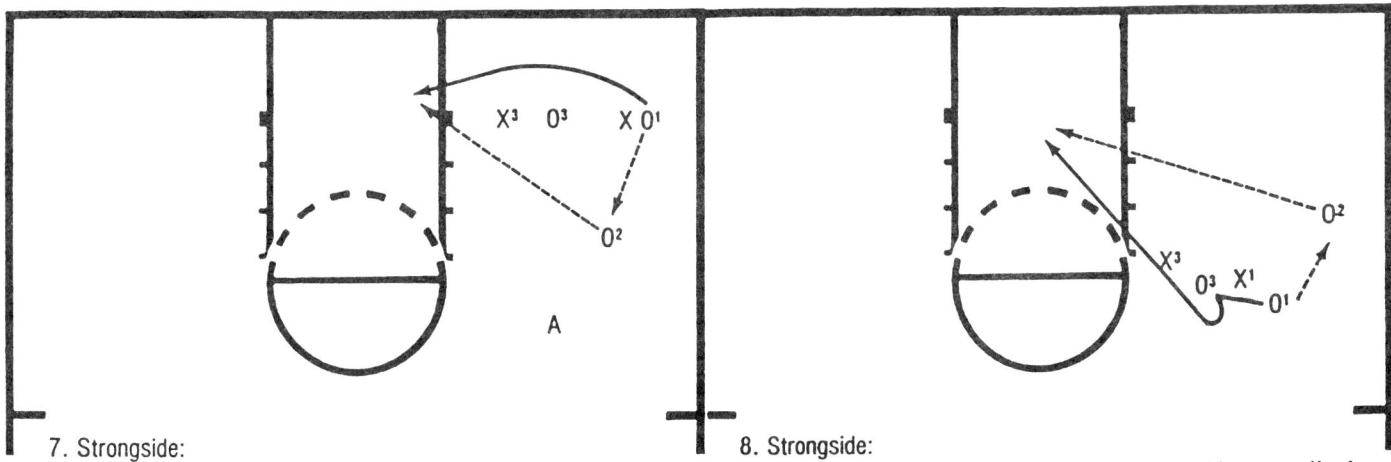

7. Strongside:
A. Utah Cut - Low: O^1 passes to O^2 then rub screen off of O^3. O^2 lobs the ball from the strongside to the weakside to O^1 (if X^3 switches on O^1, O^2 may pass directly into O^3).

8. Strongside:
B. Utah Cut - high: O^1 passes to O^2 then rubs his man off of O^3. O^2 then lobs the ball to O^1 (if X^3 switches on O^1, then O^3 pins X^1 and scoots low for the pass from O^2).

49

Centers: 8. Getting Rebounding Position and Tipping

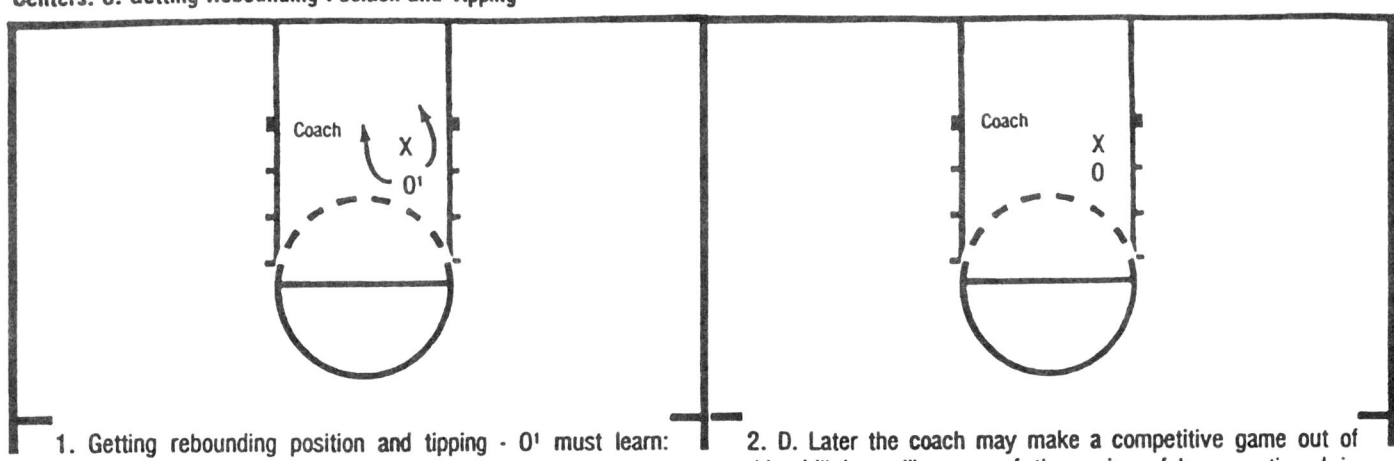

1. Getting rebounding position and tipping - O¹ must learn:
   A. Various fakes and go to the basket
   B. To reverse inside of the defensive player (X)
   C. To stutter his feet and go to the hole

2. D. Later the coach may make a competitive game out of this drill by calling one of the various fakes mentioned in A, B or C and going one point for the correct reaction to the fake called; one point for aggressively pursuing the ball. Two points for getting a rebound; and two points for putting the ball back into the basket. Game is fifteen points.

Guards

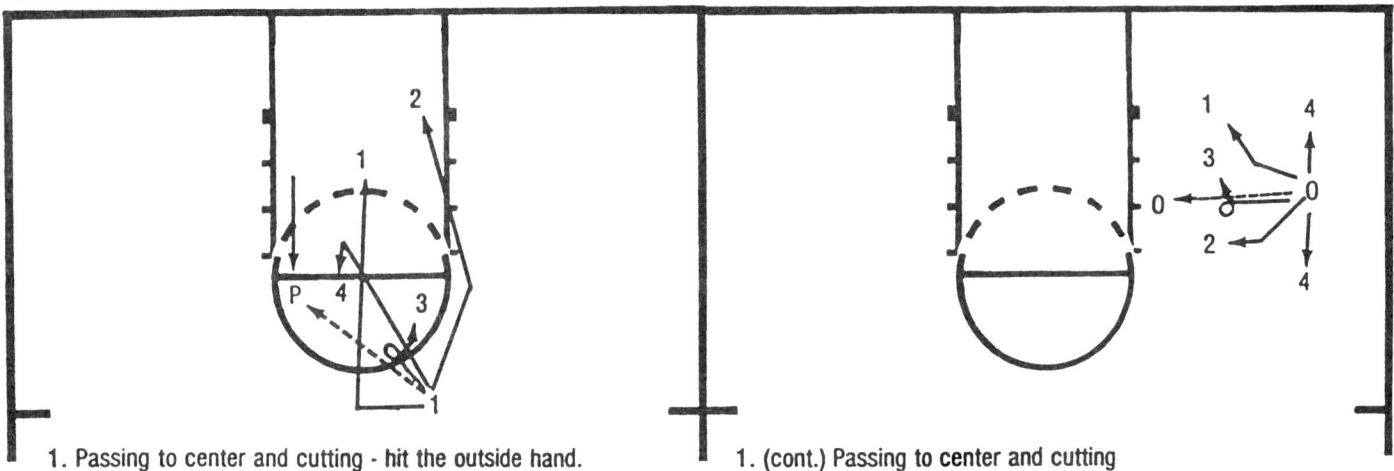

1. Passing to center and cutting - hit the outside hand.
   A. Guard dribbles - post man breaks (guard on top)
      (1). Step to the post and go
      (2). Step away from the post and go
      (3). Reverse pivot and go
      (4). Any of the above - pop back for jump shot

1. (cont.) Passing to center and cutting
   B. Low and medium post.
      (1). Step to the post and go
      (2). Step away from the post and go
      (3). Reverse pivot
      (4). Defensive man goes to the post man - drift away

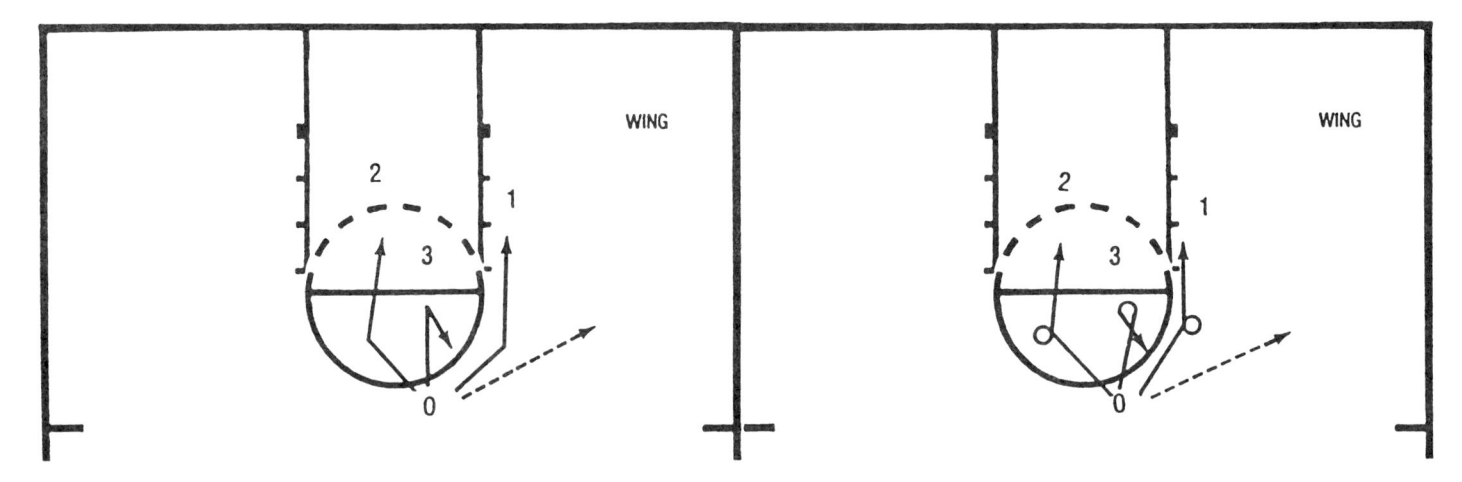

2. Passing to the wing and cutting.
   1. Step to and go
   2. Step away and go
   3. Step in and pop

3. Passing to the wing and reversing.
   1. Step to reverse away
   2. Step away and reverse to the ball
   3. Either of the above and pop back for jumper

Guards (Cont.)

4. Setting the screen for wing man or guard.
A. Guard - O^2 picks X^2 and pops back out for the ball.

4B Guard - guard pick, pop and back door. O^2 picks X^1 then must learn to pretend to pop back out for the ball and break back door for the lay up.

4C Guard screen for forward
(1). Forward with the ball (the guard must learn to roll or pop out for the shot).
(2). Forward without the ball (lateral pick is shown above).
(3). Rub screen is O^1's second option. The above diagram shows O^1 passing to M and then coming back such that O^3 can rub X^3 off his pick. Once O^1 gets the pick on X^3, he pops out to receive the ball from M.

5. Working with the forward on the side post:
A. Pass and cut to the basket
B. Dribble by and have the forward roll low for the pass
C. Dribble by and pass back to the forward for the jump shot

Forwards

1. Getting open
A. Facing the dribbler
B. Sprint out
C. Reverse in or out
Forward and guards should do this nightly to get their timing down on the back door cut.

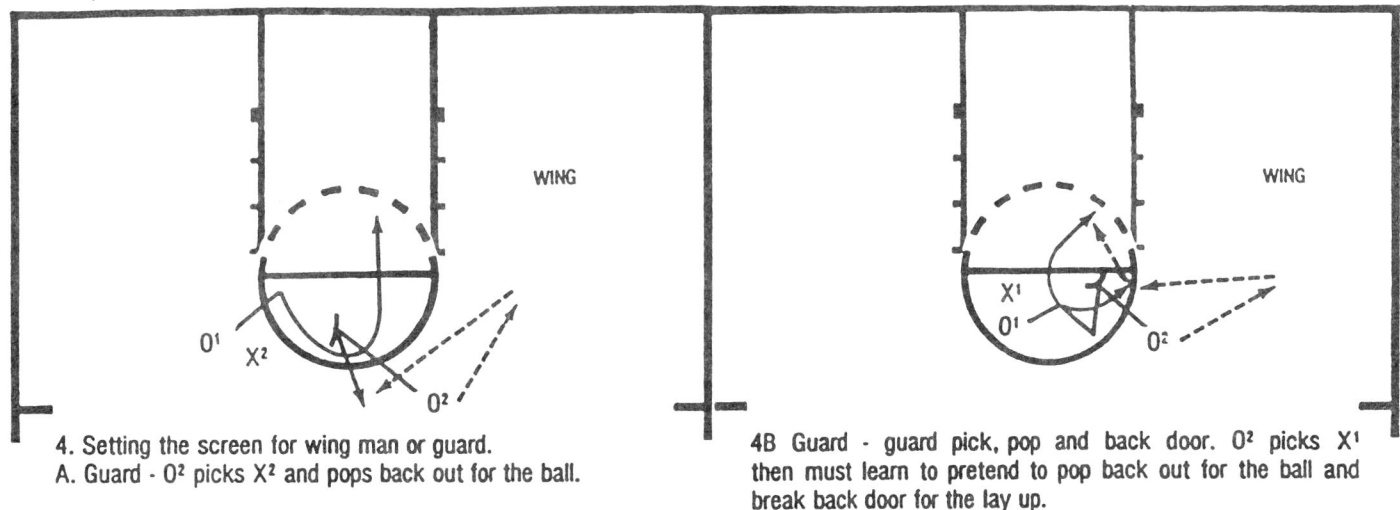

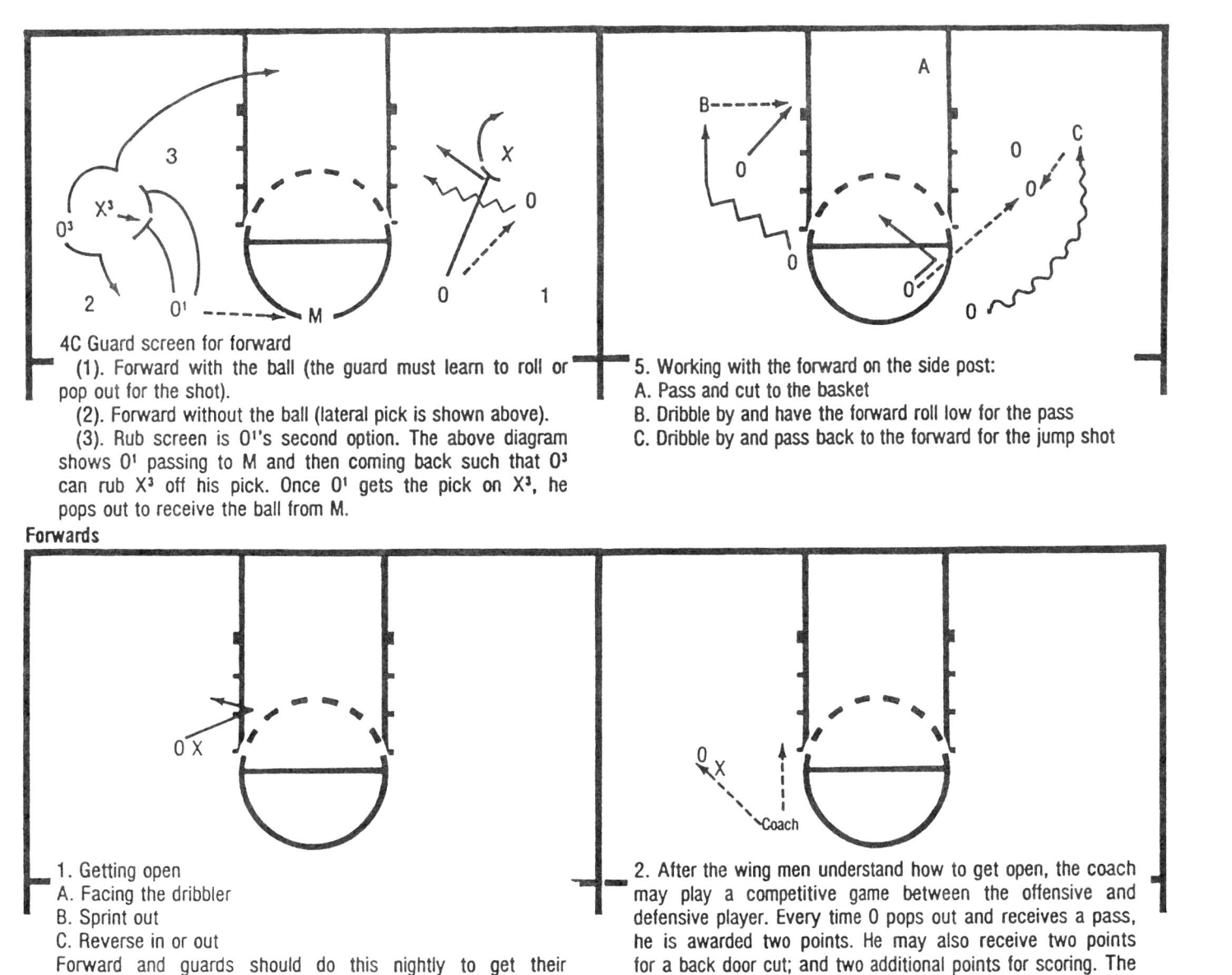

2. After the wing men understand how to get open, the coach may play a competitive game between the offensive and defensive player. Every time O pops out and receives a pass, he is awarded two points. He may also receive two points for a back door cut; and two additional points for scoring. The coach also gives the offensive player two points for proper execution of a move. The defense may score by denying a the ball for 5 seconds or by stealing the ball. Game is 12 pts.

Forward (Cont.)

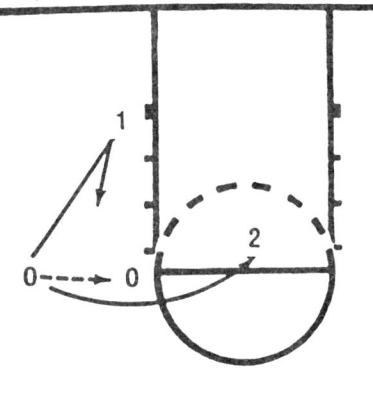

3. Passing to the center and cutting.
A. High post
  (1). Back door and pop back (reverse and straight cuts must be taught).
  (2). Over the top - rub your man off for the lay up or jump shot.

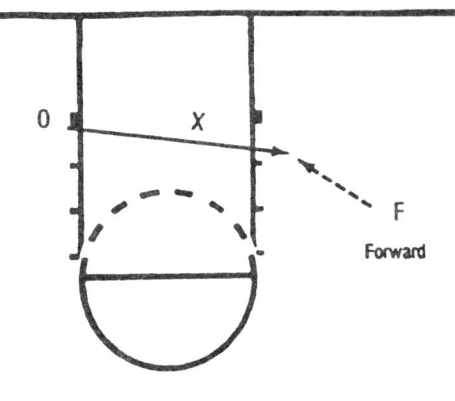

4. Passing to the post: the forward must be taught to throw away from the defensive man. X is instructed in the above diagram to play:
A. To O's low side and the forward passes to O's inside away from X.
B. to O's high side and the forward passes outside away from X.
C. Play for real, X may play either side.

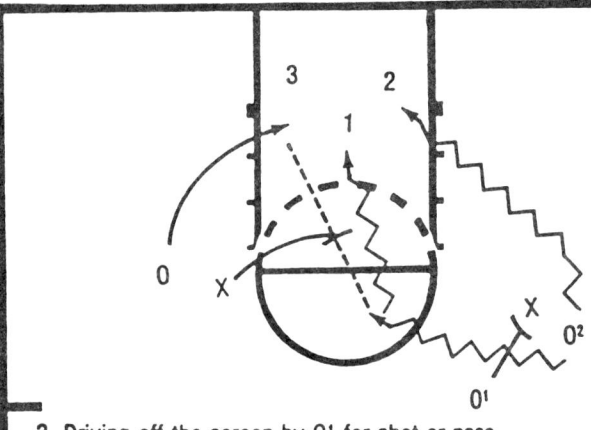

3. Driving off the screen by O¹ for shot or pass.
A. Forwards:
  (1). O² takes it to the basket or shoots the short jumper.
  (2). Explodes to the basket on fake left go right.
  (3). Hits opposite wing man as defense picks him up.
These are three seperate skill drills which need to be perfected by the forwards.

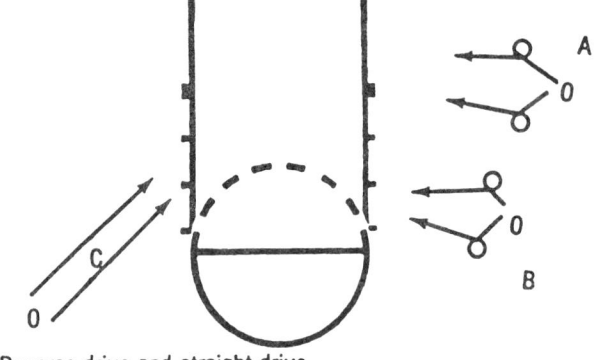

4. Reverse drive and straight drive
A. Base line
B. Inside
C. Straight drive
Drive areas are wing and corners. Players take the ball to the hole or take the jump shot.
The coach must insist that his players can perform the three drives described above. Later add adefensive player to simulate game conditions.

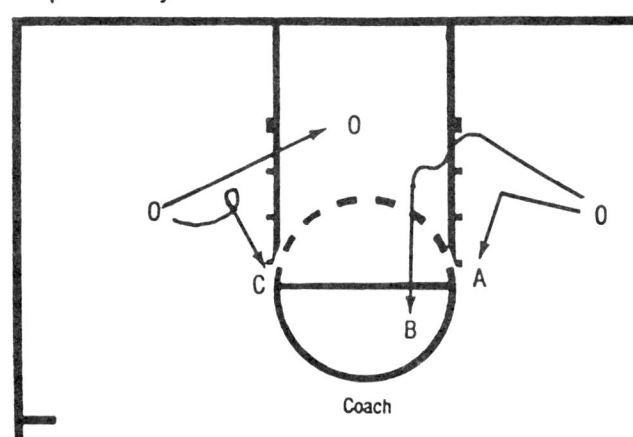

5. Getting open to receive the ball on the side post.
A. Short change of pace fakes and cuts explodes up to get to receive the ball.
B. Step behind the player on basket and explode up to receive the ball.
C. Reverse up and receive the ball.
D. Spring back door and receive the pass.

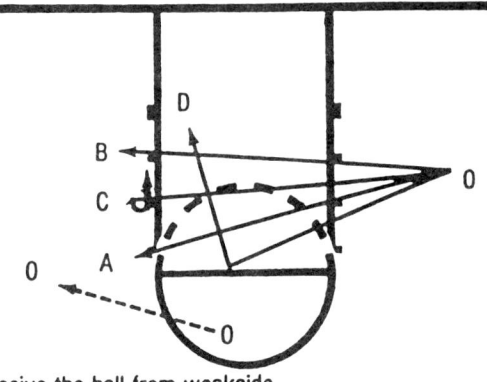

6. Receive the ball from weakside
A. Go at the man - sprint across
B. Step behind and explode
C. Reverse up or down
D. Sprint back door
E. Lob pass
  (1). Outside (2). Inside
All of these fast movements are to be taught in separate drill action.

52

Forwards (Cont.)

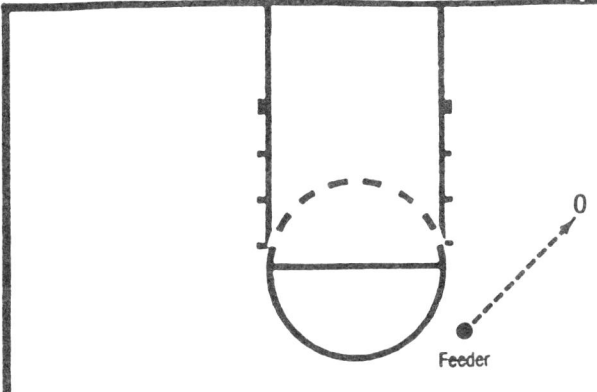

7. Offensive moves on the side post.
  A. Catch and go - reverse to the hole
  B. Fake and go
    1. Show the ball and go
    2. Drop step and go
  C. Step, fake and go
  D. Catch, turn, shoot

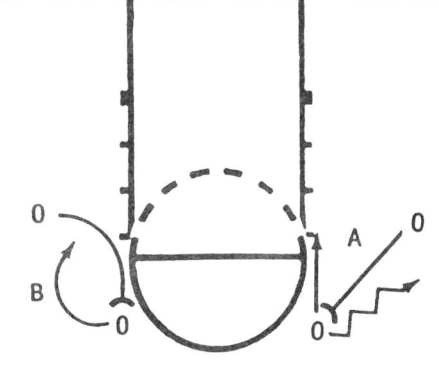

8. Screening for the guard:
  A. With the ball - pick and roll
  B. Weakside - without the ball - pick then go to the ball
The movement that is required by the forward after the pick is set is dependent on the offensive system that the coach chooses to implement. Nevertheless, the fundamentals are consistent in the above drills.

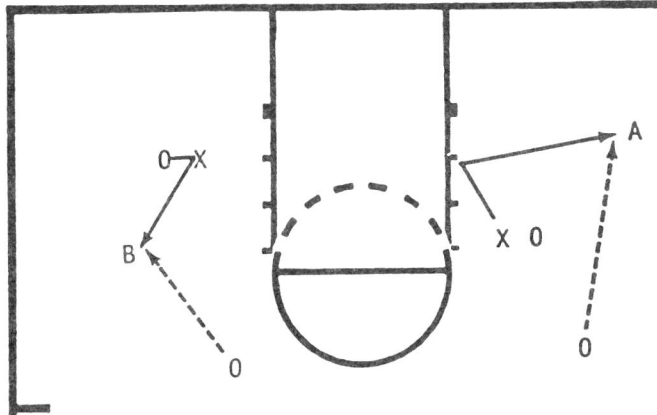

9. Keeping the defensive man busy
  A. Jab step away ("V" cut out)
  B. Jab and to the ball ("V" cut in)
  C. Drift away from the action then move to the ball - this tactic must be learned when teaching X.

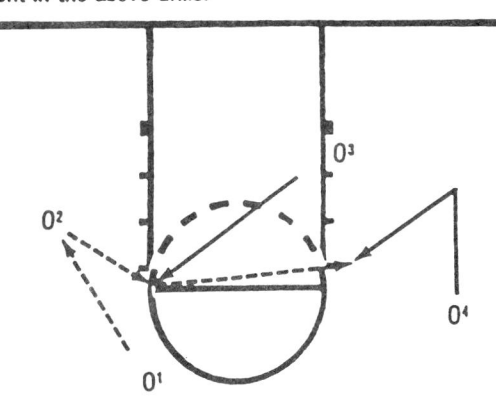

D. Drift away from the action then move to the ball. This tactic must be learned by the forward in order to free himself against a zone. In the above diagram, O^1 passes to O^2 who hits O^3 in the high post. O^4 drifts to the deep corner, but now moves to the open area once O^3 receives the ball.

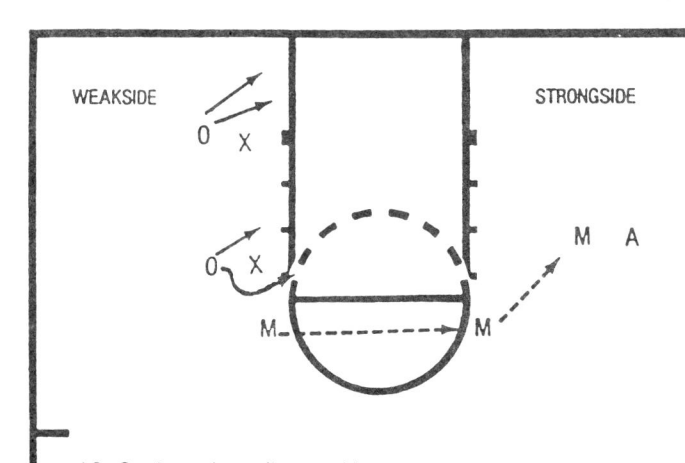

10. Getting rebounding position
  A. From weakside shot
  B. From strongside shot
This is one of the most critical skills that must be learned by the forward. The author suggests that the reader turn to the offensive rebounding drill sequence in this section.

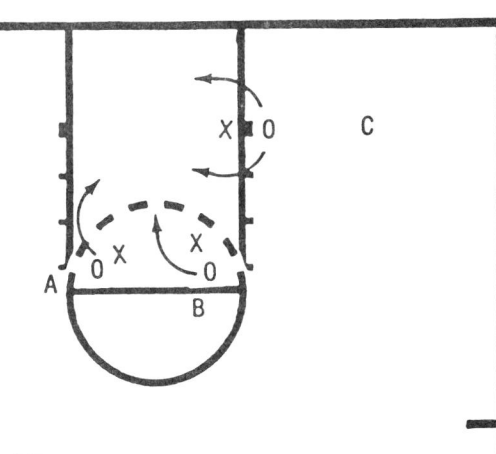

C. Keep moving drill
  A. Fake and go to the hole.
  B. Reverse inside - (instead of laying on a man)
  C. Stutter your feet and go to the hole

The coach's ability to progressively teach and maintain a high level of the "parts" offensive efficiency will be the primary factor as to how the "whole" functions.

Combining the "whole" with the "parts."

The teacher-coach now simply attaches numbers to "whole" and "part" functions. All stacks, screens, offensive footwork, passes, dribble action and rebounding (parts) must never be compromised for the numbers (whole). Therefore, we would go back to our original point of discussion and ask the team the same number series questions while continually reminding them that the numbers (whole) will not work unless the fundamental skill movements (parts) are consistently executed. For an example, a theoretical discussion of combining the whole with the parts may take place as follows:

"<u>6</u>" series - down and up picking:
1. "What are the fundamental skills that need to be executed when setting a down or an up pick?"
2. "How is timing and floor space important when setting down or up picks?"
3. "When we add a 9 to the 6 series (96), what are the critical fundamental skills (parts) that must be executed in order for the 9 to be successful?"
4. "If we are trying to free a specific player (such as 2) by using the stack (9) and up and down screens (6), what must the indicated player do fundamentally to get open? What must his teammates do to make sure that he becomes free to receive an open shot?"

This process would continue as we combine all of the base numbers 6-13 with the fundamental skills of the parts. If one is consumed by the "parts" of an offense, the timing and rhythm of the offense will suffer. If one is consumed by the "whole" of the offense, its parts will be so inefficient that the "whole" will lose function. Therefore, balance the relationship between the "whole" and the "parts" in order to have the offense at maximal efficiency.

Applying the offense to game situations.

Finally, because of its structure, the numbered motion offense increases the team's opportunity to win the contest. Within its design, the players are taught their specific roles, the definition of shot selection (high percentage or good percentage shots), and the value of individual and team discipline regarding the execution of the fundamental skills (all aspects of picking, footwork, rebounding, passing dribbling, etc.). They also learn to effectively communicate with one another, which increases the efficiency of team function (especially in relation to time and score). The author encourages the reader to refer to *Bench Coaching Offensive Strategy,* by Mel Hankinson, Championship Books Publishing Company, Ames, Iowa, for further information regarding game strategy. Once the coach and the team understands the numbers' functions, then the numbers should be added in relation to the personnel to begin building the team's offense.

In conclusion, the coach and the team <u>must</u> <u>be</u> <u>sold</u> on the numbered motion offense in order to make it function efficiently. Ogden Nash once wrote, "A man convinced against his will is of the same opinion still." Convince oneself and team that the numbered motion is the best offense invented by man. Secondly, balance the teaching of the "whole" with its "parts." Finally, identify the role of each team member and plug them into a numbered system which can be applied at the beginning, mid and end game.

Chapter 6

The Fastbreak and the Numbered Motion Offense

Chapter 6
The Fastbreak and the
Numbered Motion Offense

The numbered motion offense complements all fastbreak systems of play, whether or not the coach uses a controlled or quick tempo pace of play. In this section we will not discuss the various systems of fastbreak play: the numbered, sideline, quick player release, wing or special designate player breaking systems. Rather, we will discuss the corresponding fundamental applicable principles which occur after a made basket, missed basket or defensive steal.[1]

Basic principles that apply to the fastbreak include:

1. Proper boxing out techniques.

2. Proper rebounding release and "initial attack" techniques.

3. Proper outlet techniques:
    A. pinch post point guard release
    B. wing guard release and outlet
    C. wing-forward release and outlet
    D. wing-center release and outlet
    E. power dribble release after the rebound
    F. quick pass ahead advancement technique
    G. long pass release to:
        (1) mid court series (early game, mid game, late game, etc.)
        (2) full court series (early game, mid game, late game, etc.)

4. Mid court phase concerns:
    A. 5 men filling the lanes
    B. who's back on defense - safety man?
    C. diagonal cuts by guards
    D. non-ball handlers sprinting down court

---

[1] All three of these circumstances are conditional to time, score, strength of competing teams, illness, injuries, foul trouble, etc.

- E. ball handlers receiving the ball
- F. ball handlers dribbling or passing the ball down court
- G. special situations:
    - (1) ball handler dominated?
    - (2) ball handler trapped?
    - (3) designated trap?
    - (4) advantages lost?
    - (5) advantages gained?
    - (6) unusual game adjustments?

5. Front court phase concerns:
    - A. Immediate flow - Is everyone going where they are supposed to go?
        - (1) point guard
        - (2) shooting guard
        - (3) post high
        - (4) post low
    - B. Delay game motion - Who may we take advantage of?
        - (1) guard drive
        - (2) shooting guards
            - (a) shot
            - (b) drive
            - (c) feeds
        - (3) post high
            - (a) shot
            - (b) drive
            - (c) feeds to guards and low post
        - (4) post low
            - (a) shot
            - (b) drive
            - (c) feeds to guards and high or weak side cutting post
    - C. Motion number call (in relation to time and score)
        - (1) initial basic flow series
        - (2) crutch number flow series
        - (3) end game "nothing but winners" series

All of the basic principles that the reader is presently using with his fastbreak applies to the numbered fastbreak. Chapters 4 and 5 have identified the numbers' functions and have given us guidelines to teach the functions. Generally, if the basket is made, a number is called. However, if the basket is missed, we advance the ball up the court with immediate flow into the offense (after running our delay set). This places greater pressure on the defense because it does not give them time to set up and get organized. However, we may add some basic cautions which should be given in the transition type game:

1. Know your role. Are you doing what you are best equipped to do? If you are playing outside your role, you are hurting the team.
    A. Guard(s) are handling the ball.
    B. Forwards are passing the ball and filling the lanes.
    C. Center(s) are passing the ball and filling the lanes.
    All players are moving as quickly as possible with purpose and proper function.

2. Pressure. Immediately think "attack" once possession of the ball is gained. Physical and mental pressure should be applied on the opposition throughout the contest. If pressure is maintained for 100% of the evening, your opponents will break. The goal is to mentally demoralize your opponents with easy baskets.

3. Tempo. Run at our tempo.

4. Shot. Shoot at your tempo. All controlled teams can outsprint their opponents down the courts. However, no team needs to fly down the court and "jack" the ball up. Shot control is as, if not more, important than sprint control.
    A. Shots are always taken in relationship to:
        (1) time and score
        (2) high percentage, good percentage
        (3) one's role on the team
        (4) one's motive for taking the shot
    B. Consider how the shot affects the team mentally as well as game results.

5. Wear the defense down. All teams must be made to play defense for the entire evening. If the defensive team is not forced to play defense early in the game, when it comes

"crunch" time, the offense will be playing against a squad that has fresh legs. Also, because the numbered motion is structured to be a mental demoralizer, make the opposition play defense to "force" someone to make a defensive mistake. Often defensive errors will carry over to "lunk head" offensive play. Be patient.

6. Multiply your opportunities for success:
   A. By making high percentage passes:
      (1) feed inside
      (2) skip passes to high and low post
      (3) skip passes to weak side of the court
      (4) rarely give a big man the ball down court out of his operating areas
   B. By executing high percentage dribbling:
      (1) beware of over dribbling
      (2) beware of over penetration
      (3) beware of forcing the drive
      (4) beware of traps
      (5) be under control and know when to:
         (a) give up the ball
         (b) initiate the offense
         (c) initiate the numbers
         (d) initiate various special time and score plays

7. Multiply all team members opportunity to score by proper spacing.
   A. Keep the basket area clear.
   B. Know where one is to go on point guard penetration.
   C. Know where one is to go on wing/guard/forward penetration.
   D. Know where one is to go on center penetration.
   E. Know where one is to go on the delay break.
   F. Know where one is to go on a skip pass.
   G. Know where one is to go on a high post pass.
   H. Know where one is to go on a low post pass.
   I. Know where one is to go when various shots are taken.
   J. Know where one is to go once the number is called.

   This will increase the effectiveness of team communication and multiply one's

opportunities to score.

All of the previously mentioned material in this section is basic basketball tenants. However, the following is used by few teams because it is rarely practiced, or they have not added a communicative system which could equip their squad to effectively attack a defensive team of less than five man. For simplification, this section will be discussed from a defensive steal perspective.

The fastbreak numbered action begins once we gain possession of the ball. (Once again, the "given" in all of these defensive steal situations are time, score, shot selection, crutch plays, player roles, etc.)

1. If the offensive team has an advantage, go immediately to the basket:

    A. 1 on 0 - In most instances, the offensive player will take the wide open lay-up.

    B. 2 on 1 - Use basic fastbreak principles to score; then the numbered series:
    (1) stay wide - includes proper angle passes
    (2) get the ball in the best ball handlers possession
    (3) high percentage dribbling
    (4) high percentage passing
    (5) high percentage shots:
        (a) lay-up
        (b) short jumper
    (6) numbered options would include:
        (a) "7" - pick and roll
        (b) "70" - pass, pick and roll
        (c) "8" - give and go
        (d) "11" - would only occur if the defense had a man and a half back, and wide isolation spacing becoming valuable to one's teammate
        (e) "13" - lob pass is automatic and available of the initial break
        (f) "15" - drive, draw kick is also automatic off the initial break

    C. 3-on-1 (3-on-2), 4-on-2 (4-on-3), 5-on-3 (5-on-4)
    (1) all the basic fastbreak principles apply (passing dribbling, shooting, etc.)

(2) all the basic fastbreak delay principles apply
(3) Numbered options would include:
   (a) "6" - up and down screen
   (b) "7" - pick and roll
   (c) "8" - backdoor give and go
   (d) "9" - Most team's stacks are not a part of this transition sequence, but it can be in certain "crutch" basket situations
   (e) "10" - In transition, it is very difficult to counter by the defensive team
   (f) "11" - Isolations should always be on every offensive player's mind in the transition game. The higher the tempo, the more one-on-one mismatches will occur.
   (g) "12" - This is another automatic that will occur in the transition game. Once again, mismatches in the post and on the perimeter are created.
   (h) "13" - Lob passes are continually available in an up tempo fastbreak game.
   (i) "14" - Snapback action is continually present once the defense scurries to their recovery positions.
   (j) "15" - All offensive players should be looking to drive, draw and kick in transitions.
   (k) "16" - Pick action will confuse the retreating defense's responsibilities.
   (l) "17"/"18" - Combinations of "pick the picker" requires additional discipline and transition recovery skills of the defensive team
   (m) Most importantly, all of the combined number series are available to the offensive team once the initial and delay break options are taken. The coach must insist that self-centered offensive action will not be tolerated, because of the excellent opportunities to score off the numbered motion offense.

Once the players learn the fundamental skills associated with the numbered phase of their offense, it will enhance communication between one another and the bench. Forced offensive action such as "quick shot selection," blind passes, over dribbling, etc. will neutralize the numbered phase of the offense because the team will never get that "far" into the offense. Therefore, motion is integrated into our fastbreak offense. Also, the use of the number gives the offense a great advantage of knowing what action will be taken in the fastbreak phase of the game because it has been clearly communicated. "Move quickly, but don't hurry! <u>Use the numbers to move with purpose</u> in relationship to <u>your role</u>, the <u>time</u> and <u>score</u>."

Chapter 7

Attacking Zone Defenses with the Numbered Motion Offense

Chapter 7
Attacking Zone Defenses with
the Numbered Motion Offense

It is accurate to describe learning as a gradual process which takes place in spurts. Gradual, because intense investigation of any subject matter is tedious. In spurts, because once a concept is grasped, learning moves quickly to a new level of awareness and exploration. Such is the nature of the numbered motion offense. Once understood, the reader will add his own innovations to the most creative basketball offense in the last 20 years. Its multiplicity of uses were described earlier in the text. The offense may be used against various man to man situations (including straight, pressure, sagging, or trapping defenses), to control the tempo of the game, as a delay game, to protect a lead, to interject "crutch" plays, end-game strategic maneuvers, to adjust a basic system of play to fit specific personnel, against "freak" defenses (such as a triangle-and-two or a box-and-one sets), and most important, the numbered motion will become the most lethal weapon in the years ahead for attacking straight or match-up zone defenses. Without getting into a specific system of play, let's examine how to creatively use the numbered motion game to conceptually attack any straight or match-up zone defense:

"6" - screening up or down

1. Screening the wings down:

    A. Opens the jump shot on:
        (1) strongside - perimeter
        (2) weakside - perimeter
        (3) top of the key action
        (4) post:
            (a) inside
            (b) short corner
            (c) high and mid post

    B. Opens shots for the picker:
        (1) step out after the pick

(2) slash cut after pick

(3) post after the pick

2. Screening the wings up carries the same options described above.

3. Screening for the posts inside and outside will be discussed later in this chapter.

"62" - screening up or down for 2. The 2 man is now the designated as the primary[1] offensive player. We want 2 to take the shot unless one of his teammates have a lay-up or a "high percentage" shot. As the primary or designated shooter, 2 may take a "good percentage" shot in relationship to time and score. "2" should be receiving perimeter down screens, up screens, staggered screens, and walled screens from offensive players 1, 3, 4, and 5.

"7" - pick and roll (or pick and pop). Picks may take place on the ball or off the ball. Basic movement has the big man continually picking for the shooting guard off this movement. Against a zone, the "picker" will often become the perimeter shooter, or the dribbler off the pick will many times set up a 15 (drive, draw and kick) for a shooting teammate. This is purposed, continued pick and go action that is very difficult for the zone to defend.

1. "67" - simply adds down and up screens to the pick and roll (7) option

2. "74" - indicates that we are going to keep 5 inside (block to block) and use 4 as the designated picker. If 4 is mobile, a good shooter, or maybe 5 is much slower, the "74" permits you to maximize both players talents.

3. "742" - gives us even greater control over the play action. "742" communicates to the team that we are looking for pick and roll action (7) between 4 and 2 (42).

4. "6742" - combines the down and up screen action (6) with the pick and roll (7) for 4 and 2 (42).

---

[1] see Chapter 4, "Function of the Numbered Motion Offense," "6" screening up and down for further discussion on primary and secondary players' responsibilities.

5. "745" - means that 4 and 5 will be picking and rolling for 1, 2, and 3.

"8" - early releases on a pick and roll or a backdoor cut has limited use against zone defenses. However, it is effective motion is the team is playing a "pure" match-up.[2] Mixed cuts and passes through the "heart" of the zone can be very confusing to the defense and often result in a lay-up or wide open shot for the offensive team.

"9" - stack action involving 2, 3, or 4 offensive players on curls, pops, etc. is effective against match-ups, straight zones, and "freak defenses" for several reasons. First, the zone defensive team rarely faces any type of stack action against their opponents. Second, the stack is very difficult to match against because of the myriad of movements which may be used from the stack. Third, if the defense has some unusual character (triangle and two, box and one, or freak slides), then the <u>primary</u> shooter can be more easily freed from such defensive designs. Finally, the offense is operating "behind" the defense. This creates several problems for the defense, one of which is that the defense cannot easily see where the offensive players are and where they going. As was mentioned in an earlier chapter, the "9" series is a textbook unto itself. (The author would encourage the reader to review the "9" stack option principles described in Chapter 4, "Function of the Numbered Motion Offense.")

The 2 man may be used as the <u>designator</u> where all motion action is keyed off his initial movement, as described in Chapter 4.

1. "29" - indicates movement of the offense will begin from a double stack. Alignment, location on the floor, and designated <u>primary</u> shooters will be called by the point guard or coach.

2. "296" - initial stack movement (29) with up and down screens (6).

3. "297" - initial stack movement (29) with pick and roll action (7).

4. "298" - initial stack movement (29) with continuous backdoor action (8).

---

[2]"pure match-up" indicates that a team is playing a man-to-man zone.

5. "2962" - initial stack movement (29) with up and down screens (6) for the 2 man (2).

6. "2974" - initial stack movement (29) with pick and roll action (6) for the 4 man (4)

7. "39" - indicates initial movement of the offense will take place from a triple stack. Alignment, location on the floor, and designated primary shooters will be called by the point guard or coach.

The same series of numbers may be appropriated for triple stack action leading into: up and down screens (396), pick and roll action (397), backdoor action (398), various combinations such as "3962" (triple stack (39) into up and down screens (6) for the primary shooter (2)), or "3974" (triple stack (39) into pick and roll action (7) for player (4)).

8. "49" - indicates the initial movement of the offense is from a quadruple set. We would follow the same pattern of thinking regarding: alignment, location, and designated primary shooters, as we did in the "29" and "39" series. Similarly, the sequence numbers initiating movements would logically follow in form and function: "496," "497," "498," "4962," and "4974."

Of course, there are a preponderance of number combinations and functions which may be used with the stack series. These are to simply wet the appetite of the innovative coach.

"10" - is an effective option if the guard creating the "big on little" pick isolates the slow wing forward to be picked or the lumbering center. The defensive "point of attack" should be established from the scouting report and presented before entering the game. All stack options are viable entries to "10" ("910," "2910," "3910," and "4910"). Since "10's" nature is to "play structure oriented," limited options are available.[3]

---

[3] 10's nature - see Chapter #4, "Functions of the Numbered Motion Offense," for 10's structure.

"11" - one on one isolation action obviously cannot be done by clearing areas of the court. However, isolations can be created by 6, 7, 8, and 9 stack action as described earlier in this chapter.

"12" - horizontal or diagonal post picking (this may be from low, mid, high, or short corner positions) is <u>very</u> effective movement within the numbered motion offense. Alignment, location on the floor, and designated <u>primary</u> shooters will be called by the point guard or coach. "12R" is available if the offensive team should choose to backpick the post man (2:1:2 zone) or the weakside wing; (because the weakside wing is usually alone on the weakside low post, many coaches currently backpick him on set plays).

"9," "29," "39," "49" - all stack action is effective movement against the zone:
1. Flattening out into a 1-4 alignment is a very difficult defensive adjustment for the match-up zone.

2. Popping from the stack, then picking and posting inside is a whole series that enhances the power moves of the 4 and 5 post men.

3. After all stack action, the coach may call for post man action:
   A. "912" - (low, mid, high, corner) single stack (9), into 12 action (12)
   B. "2912" - (low, mid, high, corner) double stack (29), into 12 action (12)
   C. "3912" - (low, mid, high, corner) triple stack (39), into 12 action (12)
   D. "4912" - (low, mid, high, corner) quadruple stack (49), into 12 action (12)
   E. If the "R" is indicated, the "2912R" means after the double stack entry, there will be a reverse (back pick- R) for the post man.

"8" - back door action then flowing into "12" has limited value against straight zones, but can be effective against match-ups. The players simply mix several strong and weakside cuts with the inside power game of the 4 and 5 man in 12 action.

"7" - involvement with "7" movements were described in earlier in this chapter. Because of the nature of the zone, perimeter picking and rolling opens up driving, weakside and inside post passing option (see "7" for more information in this section).

"6" - screening up or down offers many possibilities against the zone. However, the 6 numbered motion is more effectively run if the coach slows the pick action down so as to attack specific parts of the zone:

1. "612" - would indicate targeting the wings and in many cases the post (2:1:2) and continually pick those players targeted with up and back screens. This becomes a very effective offensive maneuver when the picker begins sliding off the pick and into the heart of the zone.

2. "6125" (etc.) simply means that we will have the same pick action as described in the preceding paragraph, but we are now designating 5 for the pick action.

The possibilities to use 6 action against the zone depends on the coach's personnel and creativity. Once again, the most common error made in using the "6" numbered motion movement will be to have the players move as if they are attacking a man to man defense. Therefore, slow the movement down. Identify the targets within the zone areas. Practice picking at the various angles where the target will be located on the court. Establish a rhythm which permits picking, passing, cutting, and rebounding to function at its optimum. If the proper rhythm is not established, chaos will result. The picker, passer and shooter must be coordinated in a well-timed manner for effective function to take place.

"13" - lob pass action will usually be integrated with the 6 series described earlier. It may take place from the low, mid, high, or short corner position. Primary movement is to isolate the wing or the center post and exploit his defensive zone position. In some cases, coaches use guards to protect their weakside low position. Once this is detected by the scouting report, "13" should be used to take advantage of that weakness in the defense.

Stacks (9), backdoors (8), pick and roll (7), options have been discussed earlier and may be used for the lob. However, "6" offers "crutch" play baskets in this series:

1. "6135" - (low, mid, high, corner, wing) up and down pick (6), lob (13), for the 5

man (5).

2. "6133" - (low, mid, high, corner, wing) up and down pick (6), lob (13), for the 3 man (3).

Or the coach may add the "R" to the post to post lob action and corner weakside picking action.

If the coach has player(s) with great athletic ability, the lob (13) series can be created from the numbers. The lobs may be constructed to be used from the post, wing or short corner in most instances.

"14" - snap back action is used primarily against a man-to-man, but players will find value in its movement against various zones.

"15" - drive, draw and kick action is one of the most popular and effective offensive tactics to use against a zone defense. Players are instructed to drive the gaps, then hit the open man as the defense rotates to try and stop the driver's penetration. Although the use of more man to man zones has left fewer "gap" options, the principle of driving past one's man, being double-teamed and passing to your open teammate is a tenant of basketball that is necessary against any zone defense.

"16" - perimeter weakside or strongside blind pick action is another sequence which provides a great scoring opportunity for the offense, but it has not been effectively incorporated into a "continual attack" scheme. However, "16" provides continuous perimeter picking with "slip cuts" and pop backs which doubles the effectiveness of your zone attacks. The back screens primary function is to free the perimeter player for the jump shot, the secondary action is to look for the screener who is "popping out" after the screen or slashing toward the basket.

"17" - any combination of 7, 70, and 6 action, where 7 or 70 is followed by a 6, may be used as a special "end" or "crutch" game play. Pickers, shooters and passers must be identified by the team's specific strengths in their personnel.

"18" - is once again a special "end" or "crutch" game combination of 12 and 6, where 12 is followed by a 6. The designs of this combination were described earlier in the text; however, the reader should once again use his personnel for maximizing the effectiveness of structuring the play.

The numbered motion offense is like the Stealth Bomber in that the opposition does not know when or how it is going to hit. Once the concepts in this chapter are understood, the coach will be able to raise the team's level of attack by more effectively teaching the fundamentals needed to attack the zone and by using his personnel within their designated roles more efficiently. Also, communication between players and coach will be enhanced as to how we are going to accomplish our mission.

Chapter 8

To the Bewildered and Beguiled Critic of the Numbered Motion Offense

Chapter 8
To the Bewildered and Beguiled Critic
of the Numbered Motion Offense

Let me challenge any reader who is confused, irritated or skeptical about the value of the numbered motion offense compared with his system of play to thumb back to Chapter 4 and examine the simplicity of function of each of the numbers. The numbers are not to be memorized as separate plays, but to be learned so that the players may better understand the game of basketball. The numbering system applies to basketball as axioms apply to geometry. Rules are memorized so offensive concepts may be more easily learned. Consider the following:

1. Does the numbered motion offense help me more effectively teach fundamental skills that need to be developed in my offense?

2. Does the numbered motion offense simplify or complicate the game of basketball?

3. Does the numbered motion offense help me evaluate my personnel?

4. Does the numbered motion offense help me prescribe individualized programs to better my players offensive skills?

5. Does the numbered motion offense help the players better understand their roles within our offensive system?

6. Does the numbered motion offense increase our opportunity to have better shot selection by clearly identifying the shooters and "high percentage" and "good percentage" shots?

7. Does the numbered motion offense improve our two man game action between guards, forwards and centers?

8. Does the numbered motion offense give me more control during the motion action?

9. Is it easier to make "game adjustments" quickly and effectively by using the numbered

motion offense?

10. Is our end game action more predictable because of the clarity of communication between coaches and players as to who, what, why, when, and how we are going to execute our offense within our roles?

These are ten rhetorical questions which serve to help clarify the value and simplicity of the numbered motion game.

To the bewildered, the author recommends teaching only the base numbers of the numbered motion offense: 6 (up and down screens), 7 (pick and roll option), 8 (backdoor action), and 9 (stacks). After the coach sees the simplicity, clarity and ease by which the players pick up the system, begin to build the offense as described in Chapter 5, "Teaching the Numbered Motion Offense."

If the confused coach approaches the understanding of the numbered motion offense with the preceding paragraph's foundational concepts, five realities become evident: (1) Favorite "crutch" plays may be easily incorporated into the numbered motion offense. (2) A junior high team can run the numbered motion offense. (3) The numbered motion is a system to be built on a system. It can be used from the elementary to professional level depending on the numbers used. (4) The numbers give clarity to communication which aids the teacher-coach in evaluating and prescribing individual skill development to meet the specific needs of a player. At the same time, the numbers are used to identify and help the players understand their role within the team concept. (5) The offensive efficiency of game strategy is automatically increased. Everyone now knows who, what, where, when, why and how they are going to function individually and as a team in over-all, mid-game and end-game strategy. Therefore, tempo and the strengths and weaknesses of the defensive team is more easily exploited by an offensive team that has within its arsenal specific numbers for specific attack purposes. Let's look further at these five realities:

1. Favorite "crutch" plays may be easily incorporated into the numbered motion offense. Most coaches have a play they've been using for "x" number of years and they do not want to discard it for some "new fangled" offense. The author suggests that you <u>keep</u> your pet play! Turn to Chapter 4 which lists the base numbers of the motion offense. No matter what your "pet" play is, you will find it in those foundation numbers. Take those numbers, add them to your motion, and you have begun making the numbers a part of your system. As will be

discussed in point three in this section, do not pick random unrelated numbers or it will limit how high you can build your system. Rather, pick complimentary numbers which may build into a systematic function.

2. A junior high team can run the numbered motion offense. One's mind only becomes bewildered when he either thinks of the multitude of possible number combinations and tries to teach them too quickly or has his players memorize them as unrelated isolated numbers. The wise teacher always meets the students where they are and begins slowly to show how the numbers relate to fundamental skills they are already learning. After most of the players understand the relationship between the basic skills and the numbers, show them how the numbers may be combined to give us a more efficient offense. (Please refer to Chapter 5, "How to Teach the Numbered Motion Offense.")

3. The numbered motion is a system to be built on a system. It can be used from the elementary to professional level depending on the numbers used. Review the basic numbers: 6 (up and down screens), 7 (pick and roll option), 8 (backdoor action), 9 (stacks), 11 (isolations), 12 (post picks), 13 (lobs), and 15 (drive and kick). Is there any program in America not attempting these basic fundamental skills? If there is one, the coach should be fired because he is doing his players a great disservice by limiting their skill development. However, since it would be rare to find a coach not interested in teaching the fundamentals, turn back to Chapters 4 and 5, "The Functions of the Numbered Motion Offense" and "How to Teach the Numbered Motion Offense." These chapters will reinforce your understanding of how the numbers are put together.

4. The numbers give clarity to communication which aids the teacher-coach in evaluating and prescribing individual skill development to meet the specific needs of a player. At the same time, the numbers are used to identify and help the players understand their role within the team concept. Coaches do not want robot players, but desire players who understand what specific skills need to be improved so that the over-all offense will function more effectively. The numbers give greater "coherency" as to how the parts, which must never be neglected, may be perfected to maximize the efficiency of the "whole." As was described earlier in the text, the coach may say we are working on "nothing but 6's" and some specific deficient fundamental aspect that is not being performed up to everyone's expectations within 6's function. Once the deficiency is corrected, the coach may continue his progression in

teaching by adding the whole of the 6's ("nothing but 6's"). Once the down and up screens attain a level of proficiency, then the coach may add the stack movement (9) to the 6 action by saying "96." If the stack action is not being performed to a level of acceptance, the coach may say "nothing but 9's," and isolating the part of the 9 that needs to be corrected. Once achieved, we return to the "whole" of 96 for continued action.

By identifying the number "96" (the whole), it seems that the players are able to learn the parts (9 or 6) more rapidly, because the numbers help them relate as to how the "whole" fits with the "parts." All outstanding teachers use many methods to try to encourage students to see the "big picture" of what they are working toward. The numbers help crystalize the relationship between the whole and its parts in the numbered motion offense.

5. The offensive efficiency of game strategy is automatically increased. Everyone now knows who, what, where, when, why and how they are going to function individually and as a team in over-all, mid-game and end-game strategy. Therefore, tempo and the strengths and weakness of the defensive team is more likely to be exploited by a team that has within its arsenal specific numbers which they may use for specific purposes.

Presently, the basic motion does not offer the "squeezed to the point" options that may be employed by the numbers set. Secondly, in mid-game strategy, the coach would like to take advantage of some specific weaknesses which has developed in the course of the contest. Injuries, foul trouble, mismatches, fatigue, or a defensive player who carelessly turns his head are just a few of the nuisances which may be exploited by an offensive team if they have a precise method for attacking a vulnerable area of the defensive squad. Finally, the numbered motion offense gives the coach and team confidence and control over the end game situation. Because of the nature of the numbered options, the coach may continue to run the team's strongest offensive options against the defense's weakest designs. This type of preparation will most times result in scoring opportunities for the offensive teams.

The cynics will jeer when first exposed to the numbered motion offense: "It's too complicated" or "I'm playing with pygmy sized players who have pygmy sized brains; they'll never understand such a complicated system." The mind-set of the cynics opposed the obvious value of the wheel, and probably never adopted its use until they were run over by a wagon. If you don't use the number set described in these chapters, be cautioned of vehicles with wheels.

At the same time, the author is not naive about how most basketball games are won - by superior talent. My old coach often remarked, "You take the plays, and I'll take the players and let's play a game. The big X's will almost always pound the little O's." But the real question is, how would the "big X's" do against the numbered offense that has "big" O's?

As a body, coaches must be described as innovative conservatives. They don't like to change, but will change if a new idea can help them win games. Pragmatically the numbered motion offense may not have the same impact as the invention of the wheel, but it will help the coach and his team win basketball games!

Chapter 9

Signaling the Numbered Motion Offense

Chapter 9
Signaling the Numbered Motion Offense

Vic Bubas, the former highly successful coach at Duke University, once remarked that, "You need to be able to run your offense with a handkerchief in your mouth and one hand tied behind your back." How does the coach or players call a numbered play over the screaming voices of a packed arena? In this section, we will briefly discuss the difference between the numbered offense and the "call-a-play" offense. Then, examine various bench-play-calling techniques that have been used by various players and coaches over the years. Finally, the author will encourage the reader to develop a signaling system that they are comfortable with regarding their own numbering system.

The opportunity to call a special play usually occurs after a made-basket or a dead ball situation in the contest. But the numbered motion is predicated on continual flow, rather than on a "let's get set-up" stagnated slow tempo offense. The numbers are built into play action, two or three man games that take place as opportunities arise. For instance, if the delay break is being run and the 4 man is at the pinch post position so that he may want to run a pick and roll with the guard, he then cues the guard by calling "7". Because of the floor spacing designs of the numbered motion, the court is cleared for the guard and forward to work a two man pick-and-roll game amidst the flow. In most instances, two-man game function is enhanced because communication of the numbers has greater clarity than using other verbal calls. It is easier for the forward (4) and guard to run a pick-and-roll by the forward shouting "7" than it is for the forward to come lumbering over to the guard waving his hand and yelling, "Bob, come over here!" Therefore, the numbered motion offense is significantly different from traditional play offenses, because, in most instances, the numbers are being called in the flow of the game.

However, if the coach desires to call numbers from the bench, train your players to hear your voice in the midst of a raucous crowd. In practice sessions, use any kind of loud deafening sounds (pep bands, stereo systems, etc.) to teach your players to hear your voice through the noise. Like soldiers who hear the sergeant's command to "charge" in the midst of a clamorous battle, so may your players learn to distinguish your voice above all others. Once the player hears the "call" from the bench, he immediately echoes it to the rest of his teammates. Therefore, it is not necessary to call the plays from the bench, but it can be done if the players are taught to hear the coach's commands.

Coaches have been creative in using an incredible menagerie of methods for calling their offenses from the bench. The author does not endorse any of the following systems, but recognizes that these "offensive initiators" to motivate the reader to come up with his own method of signaling :

1. Clock technique:
    A. score tied
    B. we're ahead
    C. we're behind

2. Hand cues:
    A. one fist:
        (1) up
        (2) down
        (3) right
        (4) left
    B. two fists - same as one fist
    C. thumb up or thumb down
    D. 1 through 5 fingers
    E. open hand(s)
    F. flashing hand(s)

3. Bench placement cues:
    A. where the coach sits:
        (1) left end
        (2) right end
        (3) middle
    B. where the assistant coach sits
    C. where the manager sits

4. Baseball coach's cues:
    A. skin on skin
    B. skin to (whatever) - these are unlimited
        (1) belt
        (2) head

(3) shoulders
(4) etc.

5. Name of state cues offense

6. Name of city cues offense

7. Clipboard
   A. up
   B. down
   C. etc.

8. Designated "under the offensive basket signal caller." This person would receive his cues from the coach and pass it to the offensive team under the basket.

9. Numbered card cues:
   A. straight numbers
   B. combinations numbers

10. Colored card uses:
    A. single card color
    B. double card color
    C. triple card color

Some of these techniques seem bizarre to the author, but coaches are a diverse group of our populace and if a system "works," use it. Just as we may "over-coach" and under-teach," we may also "over-communicate," which leads to "utter-confusion." Be cautious with your signaling system. Keep it simple. The emphasis should never be on trying to understand what offensive number we are trying to execute, but how it is to be executed.

Chapter 10

Making Basketball Fun with the Numbered Motion Offense

Chapter 10
Making Basketball Fun with the
Numbered Motion Offense

Learning becomes stimulating when the teacher involves the student. Socrates used this technique to force his pupils to inductively "think through" a given subject matter. In "Making Basketball Fun with the Numbered Motion Offense," the author suggests this "Socratian method of learning." By posing open ended questions while encouraging investigative responses, the students are given the opportunity to become involved in building the offense. Following are questions that will increase the players' understanding of the offense through encouragement of their input, as well as making the number system a fun experience:

1. Establish a cause. We have the motion offense, what are some problems with the offense?
   A. spacing
   B. shot selection
   C. shot options
   D. defined roles
   E. tempo control
   F. lack of perimeter options
   G. lack of inside options
   H. the danger of it becoming a jump shot offense
   I. lack of purposed continuous action if the "crutch" play does not work
   J. the end game is filled with uncertainties regarding who will take the shot if our first few options have been stopped by the defense

2. We like to run the fast break, but there is a lack of rhythm from the time we enter the break and the time we get into our flow. How can we move from our break into our offense immediately after our fast break delay options are expired?

3. You may want to take the players directly into the offense, guiding them through discussion of the numbered motion game. The motion game can be improved by clearly defining positions, operating roles, and what to do in the early, mid, and end game phases

of the offense. Most importantly, you can communicate more clearly with one another in such a manner that it will increase your confidence level as to the efficiency by which you execute the offense. Hopefully your team will at least express interest in a solution to the objectives that have been presented. Inductively walk them through each phase of the offense, answering one question after another regarding their positional responsibilities. Assure them that they have already learned the basic fundamental skills of the motion and now you want to build the offense together in such a way that everyone will know what their teammate is doing when they are out on the court. The question and answer session may be conducted in the following manner:

A. The challenge is to put numbers on what you are already doing in the motion offense. Our positions are identified as follows: 1 - point guard, 2 - shooting guard, 3 - big guard/small forward, 4- power forward/second center, 5 - center or second/second power forward.
   (1) Who are you as a player?
       (a) 1 guard
       (b) 2 guard
       (c) 3 guard/forward
       (d) 4 forward/center
       (e) 5 center/forward
   (2) What two positions can you play?
       (a) 1 & 2 guard
       (b) 2 & 3 guard
       (c) 3 & 4 guard/forward
       (d) 4 & 5 forward/center
       (e) 5 & 4 center/forward
   (3) What is your greatest strength as a player?
   (4) What is your greatest weakness as a player?
   (5) What is your shooting range for a:
       (a) good percentage shot - made 50% of the time
       (b) high percentage shot - made 80% of the time

Progressions for Teaching Basketball by Mel Hankinson and *Basketball* by Margaret Wade with Mel Hankinson have a series of role defining charts that may be of value to the coach in identifying role positions. This is one of the most critical parts of building the offense. The players must know who he is in relationship to his skill level and how he may contribute most effectively to the team. If a player knows his role, he is more apt to work during his own time to develop his skills. This will result in a higher confidence level, permitting a greater opportunity to perform under pressure.

B. Give the players the base numbers from which to build their offensive roles:
   (1) "6" - is an up or down screen. "Are you already performing this skill in our motion offense? So if you come to set a back or down screen on me, you yell what number?"
   (2) "7" - is a pick and roll. "How do you use it in our motion set? Rather confusing, isn't it? How can we make it clearer, simpler, and assure us of a good shot?"
   (3) "8" - is a back door. "In our present motion, we have a problem with our backdoor; what is it? I understand that you make a great cut and two of your teammates are clogging the lane, taking away your wide open lay-up. What can we do as a team in 8 to open the floor and improve everyone's opportunities to cut backdoor?"
   (4) "9" - is a stack. "Where do you go on a stack? Why? Can we set up a double stack? How? Does 29 make sense? Why? How about 39 and 49? Where are you? How do you know where to go? Why?"

This type of discussion would continue from 6 to 18 until everyone has a grasp of how the numbered motion offense is related to what they were already doing in the basic motion sets.

C. Begin piecing the numbers together. Once everyone understands his role and the basic number sets, share with the players that "now the fun begins." This discussion may go something like this:
   (1) "If 6 is up and down screening, and I want to get my 2 man free, then what is a "62"? Is 2 the only player who shoots the ball if his number is called? When may 1, 3, 4, or 5 shoot the ball? What is a high percentage shot for you? What type of shot may 2 shoot in relation to time and score?"
   (2) "May I use a stack with my up and down picks? "96" May I start with a stack, then use up and down picks for my 2 man? "962" How about a double stack

then up and down picks for my 2 man? "2962"!!!"

(3) "If 7 is a pick and roll, may I use a stack to enter my pick and roll options? "97"? How about starting with a double stack? "297"? Or a triple stack? "397"? If I wanted to run a pick and roll with just my power forward, how could I call that? "74"? If I had a great power forward (4) and a great shooting guard (2), could I have them working continuous pick and roll situations? "742"? Let's add a double stack for fun. Can you do that? "29, 7, 42"?? Wow!"

This type of discussion would continue, but it should be controlled so that the squad as a whole doesn't become confused. "The eyes are the window of the mind." Once you begin getting blank-eyed stares, then you know that you have gone too far. Slow down, stay with the basic sets, the added numbers will come in due time.

D. The coach may tell the players to bring in five numbers to the next day's practice. Three <u>everyone</u> <u>must</u> <u>know</u>, two solid challenges. This will reinforce what you're teaching and help to keep from confusing the players.

E. "Stump the coach" days, where players quickly snap numbered options at the coach and he has five seconds to describe the action.

F. The "Baffler" is another fun exercise where the coach divides the squad into competitive teams. The team(s) on the sideline throw out number combinations for the team on the court to perform. If they perform the numbers to the sideline team's satisfaction, NO punishment push-ups, squad jumps, etc. are enforced. All punishment is minimal, emphasis is on quick thinking and fun learning.

G. "Mr. Perfection" is controlled by competing squads as discussed in "F", by team captains, or by the coach. Now, when a number is called, all aspects of the offense must be performed to its maximum efficiency or punishment is dealt out by the "enforcer." Again, the intent is to intensify expectation of learning the numbers, not punishing the players.

H. "Quarterback Call" is a competitive game where one coach takes the offensive team and the other takes the defensive team. The offense is given the following

contingencies for function. The coach may:
(1) use only base numbers
(2) use only base numbers freeing:
- (a) guards
- (b) posts
(3) use combination numbers for:
- (a) guards
- (b) forwards
- (c) posts
(4) use combination numbers for:
- (a) early game tempo
- (b) mid game strategy
- (c) end game strategy
(5) use combination numbers for "crutch" plays

These are very competitive games and may be controlled by the coach to have fun and build understanding and confidence in the numbered sets.

In conclusion, I'm reminded of a philosophical comment on life made by George Raveling, University of Southern California's head basketball coach: "People need to enjoy life more; after all, the alternative isn't much fun." Learning is increased if people like what they are doing. The numbered motion offense offers the coach and team the excitement of being on the cutting edge of an innovative development in the game of basketball. Let them have fun while they are creating their new offense!!!

Index

A

Ace, 12

Action, snapback, 16

Adjustment, bench, 24

Aims, 13

Alignments, offensive, 4, 15, 25

Alternatives, flexible, 7

American Stealth Bombers, 6

Angles, 8, 19, 22
  dribbling, 8
  picking, 19

Application, game, 15, 36

Areas, offensive operative, 29

Athletic ability, 32

Attacking zones, 63

B

Backdoor, 15, 17, 20

Backpick, post, 8, 15

Backscreen, fake, 17

"Baffler", 86

Ballhandlers - fastbreak, 57

Baseball cues, 81

Basic motion game, 3

Basket congestion, 21

Belief in oneself, 36

Bench Coaching - Offensive Strategy, 55

Bench cues, 80

Bench adjustments, 24

Bewildered, 74

Big guard, 16

Big on little, 15

Blind pick, 16

Blue - offensive isolation, 28

Bombers, Stealth, 6

Box and One, 64

Boxing out, 57

Breakdown of positions, 42

Bubas, Vic, 79

Building an offense, 24

Building offensive series, 15

Bumps, 17

C

Center, 16

Center's position breakdown, 42

Chalk talks, 37

Chest pass, 33

Clarity, 74

Clayton, Dale, vi

Clock technique, 80

Colored cue cards, 81

Combination defenses, 6

Combination numbers, 15, 19, 24, 26
    stacks, 24

Combining whole with parts, 54

Command, verbal, 18

Communication, 3, 11, 18, 20, 75

Concepts, understanding, 24

Conceptual numbers, 16

Confidence, 12

Confused, 74

Congestion, 2

Congestion, basket, 20

Constants, offensive, 6

Continuity, 7

Control
    motion offense, 2, 11
    offensive, 60
    tempo, 20

Convincing others, Offense, 36

Corresponding offensive angles, 22

Countering pressure, 20

Counters, 3, 12, 21

Critics, 72

Crutch plays, 2, 15, 21
Cues, 3
    hand, 80

Curls, 15, 16

Cutting moves, 2, 8
    cuts, 17
    slip, quick, 17

Cynics, 76

D

Dead ball, 3, 21

Deep shooting areas, 30

Defense to offense, 30

Defense, occupying, 8

Delay game, 58

Delay fastbreak, 2, 3

Designated shooters, 18

Designated passers, 18

Designated pickers, 2

Designator, offensive player, 22

Designed offense, 7

Developing confidence, 57

Diagonal cuts, guards, 57

Diagonal post picks, 16

Dictates, 11

Double stack combinations, 24

Double stack, 23

Double numbers, 21

Down picks, 3, 15

Draw, 16

Dribbling, 2, 8, 60

Drills for breakdown of positions
    centers, 43-50
    guards, 50-51
    forwards, 51-53

Driving, 16

Duke University, 79

Dunk, slam, 33

Dysfunctional execution, 17

E

Early release, 15

Efficiency, 4

Efficiency, offensive, 76

Ego, 7

Eight - offensive series, 15, 20

Eighteen - offensive series, 16

Elbow, 15, 26

Eleven - offensive series, 16

End game, 3, 4

Evaluate, 4, 73

Execution, dysfunctional, 17

Execution
    offensive, 11, 22
    dribbling, 60

F

Fake back screens, 16

Fastbreak offense, 6

Fastbreak into the numbered motion, 56, 57

Fifteen - offensive series, 16

Fist signaling, 23

Flex, 2

Flexible, alternatives, 7

Floor, spread, 3

Flow, offensive control, 17

Fluid transition, 3

Forced shots, 11

Forced defensive errors, 60

Forward position breakdown, 42

Forward - pick and roll, 19

Foul trouble, 57

Fourteen - offensive series, 16

Freedom, 6

Frontpick, 15

Fun, 24, 82

Function, numbered motion, 14, 15

Fundamental
    skills, 2, 7
    execution, 24

G

Game applications, 15, 36

Game situations, 54

Game adjustments, 74

Games, tight, 13

Ganging-up, 18

Give-and-go, 20

Goals, 11, 13

Guards, 16
    diagonal cuts, 57
    position breakdown, 42

Gulf War, 6

H

Hand signals, 23

Hankinson, Mel, iii, v, 55

Harris, Del, 15

High percentage passes, 60

High post, 8

High percentage dribbling, 61

High percentage shot, 3, 4

Historically, 16

Hot shooter, 3

I

Ice - isolations, 2, 15, 27

Identified numbers, 15

Immediate flow fastbreak, 58

Individual offensive moves, 2

Initiating offense, 60

Innovative, 37

Intelligent spacing, 29

Intense movement, 22

Isolations
    one-on-one, 2, 15, 27
    operative areas, 29

Inverting stacks, 21

J

Jeers, 76

K

Key to diagrams, 42

Key combinations, 27

Keys, offensive, 22

Kick-out, 16

Knight, Bob, vi, 7

Know your role, 59

Knowledge, 46

L

Lanes, fastbreak, 57

Late game shots, 20

Lay-up, 20

Leflore, Al, vi

Level talent, 18

Little on big, 15

Little, picking, 15

Location, court, 22

M

Main man, 20

Man to man or zone, 6

Married offensive positions, 23

McGregor, Douglas, 11

Memorizing motion numbers, 17

Mid motion, 11

Milwaukee Bucks, 15

Mirror movement, 22

Mismatch, 3, 18, 27

Motion offense, 22

Movement, intense, 22

Mr. Perfection, 86

Multiplicity - offensive counters, 21

N

Nash, Ogden, 55

Nature of motion offense, 5, 6

Neutralize pressure, 2

Nine - offensive series, 15

Nothing but winners, 58

Numbered motion - fastbreak, 56, 57

Numbered motion offense, 3, 24

Numbers identified, 15

Numbers sequenced, 28

O

Offense to defense, 30

Offense, 3

Offense, fastbreak, 6

Offensive strengths, 6

Offensive flow control, 11

Offensive control, 60

Offensive efficiency, 76

Offensive moves, individual, 2

One-on-one isolations, 2, 15

Operative isolations areas, 29

Order, systematic, 16

Outside motivated sources, 37

Outside-in, 18

Over-coach, 17

Overwhelmed, 37, 38

P

Pandora's box, 39

Paralyzed thinking, 24

Parts, teaching, 36

Parts, teaching, 12, 13

Pass, touch, 20

Pass, lob, 16

Passes, snapback, 61

Passing, 2, 60

Patient, 12

Patterns, offensive, 7

Paying the price, 6

Peaking, 6

Penetration, 60

Perfection, 22

Perimeter shooter, 22

Perimeter, 16

Perish, 13

Personnel, 8, 16

Philosophically - team play, 11

Pick and roll, 15

Pick the picker, 15, 16

Pickers, designated, 2
Picking, 2, 8, 29

Picks, 3
   double, 3-4
   single, 3-4
   triple, 3-4
   vertical, 3
   horizontal, 3
   diagonal, 16
   up, 3
   down, 3

Pinch post, 20

Pivot reverse, 19

Point guard, 16

Pop-in, 15

Pop-out, 15

Popular offenses, 7

Position groups, 39

Position breakdown, 42

Post positions, 20

Post locations, 20

Post rolling, 9

Post play, 8

Post picking, 16

Power forward, 16

Pressure, defense countering, 20

Pressure, offensive, 59

Pressure defense, neutralizing, 2

Pressure, dribbling against, 8

Price, paying the, 6

Primary numbers, 16

Primary player, 17

Principles, 7

Protecting a lead, 20

Proverbs, 13

Purpose, numbered motion, 10, 11

Q

Quadruple stacks, 21, 26

Quarterback Call, 86

Quick cuts, 17

Quick shot temperaments, 24

R

Raveling, George, 87

Rebounding, 2, 6, 31
    inside, 31
    perimeter, 31
    release, 57
    outlet pass, 57

Red offensive isolation, 28

Replace, 9

Reverse pivot, 19

Reverse ball, 16

Rhythmic offensive flow, 17

Role, 3, 12

Roll and pick, 15

S

Safety men, 57

Score and time, 12, 27

Scorer, 4

Scout, 8

Screen, post, 7

Screening wings, 64

Screening, 15, 17

Second guard, 16

Secondary player, 17

Secret weapon, 6

Self-belief, 36

Self-knowledge, 36

Selling the offense, 29

Sequence of numbers, 28

Set plays, 2

Seven - offensive series, 15, 19

Seventeen - offensive series, 16

Seventy - offensive series, 15, 31

Shallow shooting areas, 29

Shooters, designated, 18

Shooting, 2, 29

Short corner, 16, 20

Shot selection, 59

Shots, 3, 4, 17
    high percentage, 3, 4, 17, 18
    good percentage, 17, 18

Shuffle cuts, 21

Signaling, 23, 78, 79

Single - picks, 3

Six - offensive series, 15

Six - offensive series, 15-17

Sixteen - offensive series, 16

Sixty-two - offensive series, 17

Skills, 7

Skip passes, 61

Slam dunk, 33

Small forward, 16

Smith, Dean, vi, 7

Snapback passes, 61

Snapback action, 19, 33

Spacing, intelligent, 19, 29

Special shots, 20

Spread floor, 3, 20

Stacks, 3, 15, 23, 24
    single, 15
    double, 23
    triple, 24
    quadruple, 21

Staggered picks, 3

Star player, 27

Stealth bomber, 6

Strategically, 3

Strategy, 27

Street, Marty, vi
Strongside pick action, 33

Structure, offensive, 18

Stump the coach, 86

Systematic, 15, 16
    order, 16
    concepts, 24

T

Talent level, 18

Teaching tools, 22

Teaching the numbered motion, 35

Teamwork, 22

Temperaments, quick shot, 24

Tempo, 7, 18

Tenants of basketball, 61

Terminal offense, 6, 7

Theory X, 11

Theory Y, 11

Thinking, paralyzed, 24

Thirteen - offensive series, 16

Three point shot, 27

Tight games, 13

Time and score, 10, 27

Timing, 22

Touch pass, 20

Transition basketball, 61

Transition game, 31
Transitional phase, 3

Trapped ball handler, 58

Trapping defenses, countering, 64

Triangle and two, 64

Triple
   picks, 3
   stacks, 24

Twelve - offensive series, 16

Two man games, 2, 23

U

Under-teach, 17

Under-whelmed, 37

Understanding concepts, 24

Up picks, 3

V

V cuts, 2

Verbal command, 18

Vertical picks, 3

Vision, 13

Vulnerable defense, 3

W

Wade, Margaret, 84

Walled picks, 3, 23
War, Gulf, 6

Weak defensive player, 28

Weakness, 4, 6

Weakside pick, 16

Weapon, secret, 7, 21

Wearing the defense down, 59

Whole, teaching, 13, 56, 57

Work, 37

Worrell, Phil, vi

X

Theory X, 11

Y

Theory Y, 11

Z

Zones - offense, 8

Books by Mel Hankinson

Progressions for Teaching Basketball

Bench Coaching - Offensive Strategy

Bench Coaching - Defensive Strategy

How to Teach the Match-up Zone

Developing Championship Thinking

The Numbered Motion Offense

Writing and Publishing Your Book - A Coach's Guide

Basketball by Margaret Wade with Mel Hankinson

Motivation - the Key to Success

Motivated Athlete Personality Profile

Motivation - A Systematic Approach

The Millwright Poet

Tapes by Mel Hankinson

Teaching Offensive Basketball (70 min.)

Defensive Training (30 min.)